Dedication

To Colleen whose love and support inspires me daily and to Rich, Paul, Kris, Abby, Chris and Laurel who are my constant reminder why we make leadership a way of life for their future!

Printed in the United States of America
First Printing 2019

ISBN-13: 978-0-578-48893-6

RPC Books
www.rpcleadershipassociates.com

A Branded Imprint of

RPC Books
rpcleadershipassociates.com

Acknowlegments

Successful business books, like successful leaders, do not happen by chance. This one evolved over the last five years to become the version you are reading now. It is solely based on the candid feedback and insights on the best articles and stories from clients, prospects, readers, students, and supporters of the RPC Leadership Associates, Inc. Vision to make Leadership a Way of Life. This is a book about them!

I once again called on a very talented group of professionals to help make this, our sixth book together, a reality. As with the previous five books, each team member took on a piece of the project as if it were their own. The editing by Danielle Willis proved invaluable to create a great finished product. The cover graphics from Paul Feith at Paul Gregory Media helped set the tone for the stories told between the covers. His collaboration with Jeff Ross of Ross Creative Works created the winning formula for the cover graphics. Julia Newton at Archer Media Services created the layout to optimize the overall experience for the reader. It feels great knowing we have this team supporting our publishing efforts. They make it look and feel easier than I am sure it is, and I cannot thank them enough for their support over these past eight years together!

And finally, I cannot thank my family enough for their ongoing unconditional support, patience, and insight. Everyone helped in some way to bring it all together, and you continue to inspire me!

Thank You!

Table of Contents

Table of Contents (continued)

Table of Contents (continued)

Introduction

When RPC Leadership Associates, Inc. was created in July 2008, we set out to update the way leadership and leadership development was conceived and executed across the small and mid-sized for-profit and non-profit landscape. A key element of our Vision and Strategy was to approach leadership development from an attitudinal perspective. We believe leaders must think like leaders before they can become leaders, regardless of what it says on their business card! While this concept sounds simple and straightforward, it is anything but in practice.

In the years since we started, several key messages evolved through our work with corporate leadership teams, individual professionals, entrepreneurs, business owners, and non-profit leaders. Phrases like "Hope is Not a Strategy," "What you Believe you Think and what you Think you Do," and "Well Done is better than Well Said" represented our earlier work. In the last five years, we've also added staples such as "Trying to be Perfect...or Excellent," "There are seven days in the week...Someday is not one of them," and " Adapt or Die" representing the sustainable success our clients achieved by first "thinking" like leaders and then naturally becoming more effective leaders.

In those same years, we continued to write monthly articles about what it takes to think like a leader and addressed topics that were top-of-mind for our clients, prospects, and readers. Based on their feedback, we took the best ideas from those articles, combining them with five new, never before published ideas and created *I'm Still Sayin'... More Revelations for Making Leadership a Way of Life.*

No matter where you open this book, there is an idea related to the attitudinal aspect of leadership. Within these 52 quick-read ideas lays the foundation for your own continuous journey to making Leadership a Way of Life. Read them once a week or read many at one time. But don't just read them! Read them and apply them in the context of your own leadership situation!

Enjoy the Book!

Section I:
Personal Leadership

"Personal leadership is the process of keeping your vision and values before you and aligning your life to be congruent with them"

~ Stephen Covey

Leadership starts with leading ourselves. If we cannot effectively lead ourselves, we have little right to ask others to follow us anywhere. This section is about the things we need to embrace to effectively think like and, ultimately, behave like lifelong leaders!

Section I: Personal Leadership

There are 7 days in the week...
and "Someday" is not one of them!

I often hear leaders talk about what they are thinking about doing with their businesses in the next year. The conversation is a great opening for discussions on execution and, at the same time, the execution-killer: Procrastination!

We all know about procrastination because we all do it. At some point in our careers, we put off something that was important in one way or another. We knew what we needed to do was important, and yet we put it off anyway. So why do we put off goals we know are important to do something else? In our experience, we see three main drivers of procrastination.

✔ **Laziness** – I am not suggesting for a minute that business leaders are lazy. What I am suggesting is that we are being lazy when we avoid an important task we don't like by filling time with an unimportant one. Brian Tracy speaks to this phenomenon when in his book *Eat That Frog!*. He suggests doing the hard thing (or the thing you don't like to do) first so the rest of the day is free from the stress of needing to do that thing.

✔ **Apathy** –When we repeatedly put off a task we once thought was important until we can put it off no longer it, apathy has set in. If we put it off this long, was the goal really that important? In the absence of another priority that took its place, the answer is likely no, it wasn't. To prevent apathy from setting in, we identify a goal's importance relative to other goals by writing down the Rewards and Consequences of the Goal.

Section I: Personal Leadership

✔ **Fear** – Actually, when I say fear, I mean FEAR (False Expectations Appearing Real). Much of what we fear as leaders is failure. Yet, we typically fear failure without truly understanding the role it has in our learning process. We fear the unknown, though, statistically, only 8% of what we fear actually happens; and half of that is of little consequence! This fear is also the reason we identify potential obstacles early in the goal planning process so the unknown becomes as tangible as possible and we can proactively identify ways to mitigate it.

How are you keeping "Someday" out of your mindset?

Lead Well!

Section I: Personal Leadership

"Yesterday I was clever, so I wanted to change the world...
Today I am wise, so I am changing myself"

We live in a world of constant change. Still, we don't have to look far for areas that could use, or flat out need, a change in the way they operate. In several decades of experience coaching leaders through change, one of most common themes we coach against is the idea that change needs to happen somewhere else or by someone else, basically anyplace but near me! That is why the title quote from Rumi is appropriate for this discussion in that it places the onus for effective change squarely where it needs to start...with us!

When discussing the value of coaching with a prospect, one of the points I make is that, as a coach, my job is to question the answers as opposed to answering the questions. My job is also to ask the questions they won't ask themselves. It's human nature to avoid the tough questions, especially if there is an easy way to divert the spotlight to another party or part of the business.

An example of this conversation might sound like:

- ✔ **Me:** What is the biggest challenge or obstacle preventing you from achieving the desired results of your organization?

- ✔ **Them:** I keep telling the team to do things differently, and they don't get it.

- ✔ **Me:** What are you doing differently to influence that new result?

- ✔ **Them:** I try telling them what to do in different ways to help them understand.

- ✔ **Me:** Then what are you doing differently to influence that new result?

- ✔ **Them:** I've had to be more direct with what I want from them.

- ✔ **Me:** What are YOU doing...
  You get the idea.

Section I: Personal Leadership

I've had this conversation many times, especially in the last ten years as the complexities of leadership increase with constant industry disruptions and a workforce with varying expectations – to the point of being fickle! The objective is to get the leader to realize that they are the starting point for effective change. Yes, others may have to change, but that is not where it starts. It starts with the leader looking in the mirror and deciding what changes they need to make to set the tone for the attitudes and behaviors they expect from their team.

One of the most effective ways to summarize this idea is the Betari Box. The Betari Box is a circular model that shows the relationship between attitudes and behaviors in a way that clearly demonstrates how leaders, by changing their own attitudes and, as a result, their behaviors, can influence other's attitudes and behaviors. Once attitudes and behaviors are aligned to the needed changes, the rest will fall into place!

How wise are you to change where it matters most?

Lead Well!

Section I: Personal Leadership

There is never enough time to do something right…
but always enough time to do it again!

During my corporate career, we used to joke that anything that began with "re…" was a bad thing. Specifically, we were referring to re-engineering, re-work, re-bid, etc. The premise was to keep our focus on doing what we needed to do the right way from the beginning. While the concept seems so obvious, it amazes me how leaders continue to struggle to avoid the re-peat performance!

Based on my own experience with leaders across many different types of organizations, there are three key ideas to address this challenge of getting it right the first time: Dealing with Time Pressures, Making Good B+ Decisions, and Understanding the Context of the Business. Let's take a deeper look at how dealing with each one helps optimize doing it right the first time.

- ✔ **Dealing with Time Pressures** ~ Time pressures are very real! Gone are the days when we might have had the ability to get everything on our to-do list completed. The time management skill that prevails in today's business environment is the ability to get the most important things done. The ability to prioritize the activities and decisions needed to move forward while minimizing the risk of taking any steps backward (doing something again) is crucial to sustainable success.

- ✔ **Making Good B+ Decisions** ~ To keep up with time pressures, leaders must get comfortable making the right decisions without the luxury of having all the information available to them. The world simply will not slow down to give leaders more time to make the decisions. Therefore, the decisions made quickly must still be the right decisions. The biggest obstacle is generally not the availability of information, but the leader's hesitance regarding the risk (real or perceived) of making a decision without all of the information.

Section I: Personal Leadership

✓ **Understanding the Context of the Business ~** To overcome the risk of a wrong decision, leaders must have systems in place to fully understand the ongoing context of their business. We live in an information (content) rich, knowledge (context) poor world. Ignoring the contextual elements of the business until a crucial decision is needed puts the leader at greater risk of making a poor decision and elevates the likelihood of re-work. Getting it right the first time means always understanding the context of the business.

Making the time to do something again because it was not done right the first time costs the business resources in very tangible terms. The time required to do it again is time spent not doing new things to grow the business. The cost of doing anything multiple times has a very measurable impact to profitability.

How are you getting your business right the first time?

Lead Well!

Section I: Personal Leadership

"Discovery consists in seeing what everyone else has seen... and thinking what no one else has thought."

This idea posed by Albert Szent-Gyorgyi, a Hungarian Biochemist who won the 1937 Nobel Prize for Medicine, is one of my go-to quotes whenever I need to re-energize my mindset. It reminds me that it is not what people see that drives their behaviors as much as it is what they are thinking (their attitude). In the world of constant change, our leadership attitudes are that which will determine our success as leaders regardless of profession, status, or industry.

Why is this concept so important? By way of example, let's look back at any inspirational story we have heard or read about someone who was diagnosed with a debilitating or terminal affliction. The diagnosis of the affliction is usually clear and is generally accompanied with a grim prognosis, "You will never (fill in the blank)" again.. The inspiration comes from the person accepting the diagnosis, but rejecting the inevitability of the prognosis. Instead, because of their own mindset, they take a different, more positive approach and are optimistic in spite of the diagnosis.

What does this tell us about being an effective 21st Century leader? Conventional wisdom, much like a typical medical prognosis, is subject to our own attitudes and mindset. Leaders who subscribe to conventional wisdom will likely end up following, not leading, because they buy into "You can't..." or "You shouldn't..." or "You'll fail if you do that..." language. James Baldwin once said, "Those who say it can't be done are usually interrupted by others doing it." Leaders must constantly be of the mindset that whatever they are doing now is, at some point in the near future, going to be challenged – or even made obsolete – by others on the global market and adapt quickly!

How, then, does a leader adapt quickly and not fall victim to the prevailing conventional wisdom they are surrounded by? First and foremost, they need to check their own attitudes about their business and their leadership in that business. Do business owners have a Board of Advisors or a trusted Mastermind Group to check themselves against? Do the non-profit Executive Directors have the kind of people on, and relationships with, their Board of Directors to keep them honest about their own mindsets? And do corporate leaders enable a culture that encourages engagement by their leadership teams to ensure transparency and authentic conversation about the business? If the answer is 'no' to any of these questions, the leader must take steps to ensure they do not let their own perceptions and attitudes become a potential obstacle to their organization's sustainable success.

At some point or another, all leaders encounter a moment where their previous assumptions and attitudes conflict with the current reality of the business. The challenge is whether they are open to thinking differently about that which everyone else sees.

How are you thinking differently about your business today?

Lead Well!

Section I: Personal Leadership

"Don't make excuses…
make changes."

I came across this quote in a recent book I was reading called *Hacking Leadership* by Mike Myatt. It is mentioned in the context of hacking the status quo. II was struck by how straightforward a statement it was yet so telling and powerful in its underlying message. It also got me thinking about how many leaders get derailed with excuses rather than making the changes necessary for their businesses. Just as troubling are the leaders who accept excuses from their teams when changes are not effectively executed.

By most definitions, excuses are used to deflect accountability. They are typically not factual or logical and may be only remotely related to the actual issue (who hasn't heard "my dog ate it"?!). Excuses don't exist in nature and are created by humans to rationalize their own accountability gaps. There is no greater environment for accountability to falter than during times of change. Change is risky, and, unfortunately, most of humanity is looking for stability, not change, in their lives.

So how does a leader see through the excuses from themselves or their teams and stay focused on the goal? From my own experience, I submit there are at least three ways to keep the excuses from interfering with the goal. By way of example, let's use a typical situation where there are not enough resources on hand to complete a project by its original due date.

✔ **Stay on the facts of the situation** ~ If we accept reasons like, "There are no resources available, so we can't finish the project on time," as a factual without probing further, then we are allowing excuses to impede progress. General statements can be quickly validated and verified by asking about exact quantities or conversations to ensure correct actions were at least attempted.

✓ **Listen for first-person engagement** ~ A statement like, "There are no resources available, so we can't finish the project on time," doesn't include what the speaker did personally to try to resolve the shortage. Ask specific questions regarding what the person did to verify or validate the shortage through their own personal engagement. Hold them accountable sans excuses.

✓ **Focus on the goal** ~ Allowing a statement like, "There are no resources available, so we can't finish the project on time," to land without redirecting to alternatives to accomplish the goal is irresponsible. People often get hung up on the obstacles and forget to ask about, or consider, alternatives. Focusing the discussion on the goal versus the obstacle generally yields an alternative the obstacle.

Change is constant and so is the opportunity for excuses to permeate our daily leadership. Recognizing how to effectively communicate through the excuses generates the desired results necessary for sustainable success!

What excuses are holding your business back?

Lead Well!

Section I: Personal Leadership

*"Secure your mask on first...
and then assist the other person."*

Those of us who frequently travel by plane recognize these words from the flight attendants' pre-flight instructions to the assembled passengers. Those of us who prefer flying with Southwest Airlines have even heard comedic versions such as putting your mask on first "before assisting your favorite child!" In any case, the message is clear: take care of yourself first!

As leaders approach their goal setting, I will say the same thing I have to every leader responsible for a team, business, group, or project: take care of yourself first! To be clear, this is not permission to be a self-centered leader or to put yourself on a pedestal. It is quite the opposite. Here is what it does mean:

- ✔ **In order to give 100%, you have to be 100% ~** I coach several solopreneur business owners who provide services to their clients (coaches, consultants, accountants, etc.). "I do not have time to take care of myself because I am so busy taking care of clients," is a common refrain. As we talk about how tired, stressed, and frustrated they are, we land on the same question, "If you are the service you provide, by not taking care of yourself, what is the real quality of your services?" No successful business consciously sets out to provide poor service. Yet by not taking care of yourself, that is essentially the resulting outcome!

- ✔ **Physical exercise stimulates mental health ~** We all get to points where we feel mentally lethargic. The question is: what can we do about it? I find the best response is to get physical, which in my case means going for a run or jumping on the bike for a ride. If that's not your thing, find something that will get your heart rate up several times a week. Whatever activity you choose, the science is clear on the connection between your physical and mental health; both are necessary to be sustainable leaders!

Section I: Personal Leadership

- ✓ **Let you be the example for your team** ~ While the first two points focus on the leader as a person, this one addresses the value of a leader to their team. Arguably, one of the most important aspects of leadership is creating an effective team to achieve desired results. Getting 100% out of 100% of our team requires, among other things, setting the right example of personal leadership. Making personal care an important element for every person on the team means everyone is capable of doing their part to succeed as a team. Look at any sustainable successful team in any field (business, military, sports, etc.) and you will see successful personal leadership across the entire team, not just in a few members!

Truly successful leaders serve their followers. However, they do not do it at the expense of their own personal health because they know the importance of being present for their team over the long haul. When needed most, these leaders know their own physical and mental health will help them give 100% to their followers 100% of the time.

What level of service are you giving your stakeholders?

Lead Well!

Section I: Personal Leadership

Are you trying to be perfect...
or excellent?

I only ask because I have run across this question quite a bit lately. The conversation usually begins with the leader discussing how they are trying to complete a multitude of actions to advance their business. As frustration builds when it becomes evident they cannot accomplish it all, the obvious question of priorities takes center stage. Of course, prioritizing means that something will not get done, which brings us to the title question. Are you trying to be perfect or are you trying to be excellent?

To highlight the question, I often tell the story of two campers whose campsite is approached by a bear. One camper takes off running in the opposite direction while the other camper calmly takes off his boots and starts putting on running shoes. Seeing this, the first camper yells back, "What are you doing, the bear is approaching?" To which the second camper replies, "I don't need to outrun the bear, I just need to outrun you!"

Thriving as a 21st Century leader demands excellence, which is clearly not the same as perfection. You can be the best and not be perfect, but striving for perfection can be a detriment to achieving excellence at all. The difference is the leader's attitude!

Leaders who aspire to excellence know they do not need to have all the answers to successfully lead. They know the best leadership compliment they can receive is to witness their teams routinely succeed in everything they do; with or without their leader! Excellent leaders portray a contagious positive attitude and embrace the goal of being the best without the burden of trying to be perfect.

Leaders who aspire for perfection are constantly trying to achieve something that is, at best, fleeting if not impossible. These leaders are reticent to show any sign of weakness, often to the detriment of their own personal health. They focus on processes and rules as if they were leading machines that could be calibrated for perfection. In essence, they are managers hoping that by being flawless, they somehow outrun the bear. What they lose sight of is the fact the bear will always be there!

It amazes me when leaders who know perfection is not achievable justify the pursuit of it with statements such as, "I aim for perfection to keep myself motivated" or "Getting close to perfect is the challenge" to which I reply, "for who? You or your team?" Better to aim high for a level of excellence that is both achievable and focuses on sustainable success!

How do you define your excellence as a leader?

Lead Well!

Section I: Personal Leadership

"Beware the lollipop of mediocrity...
lick it once and you will suck forever."

"Average," "Par," "Mediocre," "Safe," etc. There are many words we use to describe middle-of-the-road thinking and actions. We see it in the traditional bell curve as well as the *"Diffusion of Innovation"* curve that Simon Sinek speaks about in his now famous TED Talk on *Starting with Why*. Being a successful 21st Century leader means getting out ahead of middle-of-the-road thinking by not even considering it in the first place. As Brian Wilson, philosophical music leader of the Beach Boys, says in the title quote, once you are satisfied with ordinary, it is hard to be and do special things!

How do leaders avoid licking the lollipop of mediocrity? How do they eschew the comfort of ordinary and lead others to a new, compelling, special place? How does a leader overcome the inertia of the status quo to keep their organization ahead of change to avoid being victims of change? In my experience, there are three key components to effective leadership that helps them stay ahead of the curve:

- ✔ **A Sense of Purpose** is the key component for a successful 21st Century leader to embrace. In a constantly changing business (for profit, non-profit, large, or small) a meaningful purpose is rarely about staying under the radar or middle of the pack. Sense of Purpose is about stepping to the front and communicating a compelling purpose with conviction to all affected stakeholders. A compelling purpose emboldens the entire business organization to reach new levels of effectiveness more than giving any directive could.

- ✔ **An Attitude of Adaptability** is what brings the compelling purpose to life as something unique and different for the greater good. To keep me out of middle-of-the-road thinking in my own business, I am still driven by asking and answering two of my favorite questions, variations of "What if...?" and "Why not...?" The

Section I: Personal Leadership

answers they generate help promote an Attitude of Adaptability. Because an attitude takes time to mold, it is through repetition that an effective leader develops an attitude that truly makes change a constant in their leadership and associated culture.

✓ **Embracing Risk** is a key benefit of a strong attitude of adaptability. Leading from the front and not going along with the masses is risky. Change, progress, and compelling results all typically occur at the outer edge of one's comfort zone. Effective leaders are comfortable with being uncomfortable because they understand and embrace change as a means to fulfill their purpose. The more leaders are able to embrace change on a regular basis, the more comfortable they become in adapting to the dynamic world around them. At some point, what looks risky to a manager resistant to change looks routine to a leader who is comfortable with change!

The lollipop of mediocrity looks tasty, sweet, and tempting to eat. Just ask those who try resisting county fair or carnival food (can you say elephant ears?!). I also believe those who fall in the middle-of-the-road are looking to follow those leaders of all ages and potential willing to step to the front of the line, ahead of the pack, and outside their comfort zone to lead them.

Will they be looking for you out there?

Lead Well!

Section I: Personal Leadership

The past is a point of reference...
not a place of residence.

"Comfortable," "Predictable," "Known," and "Familiar" are all terms we would like to describe our lives as leaders. Or would we? It is easy to rely on the past because it has already happened, something we have already seen and with which we are familiar. The problem is that the past is what was and is not likely a good reflection of what will be. The question becomes how do we effectively use the past as a learning experience without allowing ourselves to get "stuck" living in it?

✔ **Using the Past as a Point of Reference** ~ We are all products of our past regardless of what that past looked like. It molds us into who we are due to its influence on the beliefs and attitudes that drive our daily actions. The key to learning from our past is to get beyond remembering only what happened in the past, what I call our "Content Past." We remember events, people, and conversations from our past that we file away under "I will want to do more of that" or "I'll never work with that person again" or any of thousands of reference points. However, we need to take this a step further and consciously ask ourselves, "What did I learn from this experience?" This is what I call our "Contextual Past." Identifying the causes and effects of these experiences help us understand that a failure in the past can change a "I will never do that again" to a more meaningful, "It did not work this time due to the conditions but could work under different conditions." The reverse is also true and potentially more blinding. A success in the past should not result in a "I will always do it this way going forward" rather, a more effective, "It worked under these conditions, but if these conditions change, it might not work as well, or not at all."

✔ **Avoiding the Past as a Place of Residence** ~Living in the past, while comforting in the moment, is a dangerous place for leaders needing to stay relevant in a constantly changing world. The best way to avoid falling into this trap lies in creating and maintaining an Attitude of Adaptability to complement your Purpose. Our behaviors are a reflection of our beliefs and attitudes, which are habits of thought. By embracing adaptability as an inherent element of how we think, we consciously engage in actions that are relevant to current conditions in our life as a leader (personal, business, community, etc.). These actions can come across as contrarian and confusing to those who still embrace the status quo (read: most of your followers!). However, it is imperative that adaptability as a norm is ingrained into the psyche of the leader and the organizations they lead. In the words of Marshall Goldsmith's book title, What got you here won't get you there!

Our opportunity as leaders is to honestly assess what we learned from our contextual past and, with an open mind, create a future that leverages that new learning for sustainable success!

How will your future look different than your past?

Lead Well!

Section I: Personal Leadership

*"To attain knowledge, add things every day...
to attain wisdom, remove things every day."*

Even though leaders understand the folly of trying to fit ten pounds of "stuff" in a five-pound bag, they always seem to try it, ultimately leading to frustration and stress. When speaking with audiences, prospects, and clients regarding time management, we invariably get to the question, "What are you going to stop doing so that you can do these other new things you need to do?" Unfortunately, the most common response, either verbally or non-verbally is, "What do you mean?" To that, I say, "What I mean!"

I had the opportunity recently to visit Gettysburg National Park with my wife. Being a Civil War enthusiast, we were excited to visit the site of the pivotal turning point in the war. Prominently painted on a wall in one of the exhibits is the quote, "It is hard for the old slaveholding spirit to die. But die it must," Sojourner Truth, October 1865. Notice her quote speaks to the spirit, not the behavior, because it is the spirit and attitude that drives a leader's behavior. Thus, the first thing a leader must address when looking at change is their attitude towards managing their growth and development by effectively deciding what they will keep doing and, just as important, what they will stop doing.

- ✓ **"Just don't add anything new"** ~ Taking this approach to the challenge misses the crucial point. As outlined in the first line of Lao Tzu's quote in the title, to grow their knowledge leaders must add new things daily to keep up with today's ever-changing business environment! To choose not to add anything new because their plate is full immediately puts them on a path to irrelevance!

- ✓ **"Delegate what I don't want/can't do anymore"** ~ Once again, this approach misses the point. Creating wisdom by removing things does not imply giving them to someone else. When leaders merely move things off of their plate onto someone else's on the team, the total of the work being done doesn't change; the team is still working on things that shouldn't be there at all. There is an exception to this: when the leader gives a team member something from their scope of responsibility that directly adds to the knowledge of the recipient. This scenario should be explicitly communicated so both are clear on the purpose of the move!

✓ **"Why are we still doing this?"** ~ This is the key question leaders use to set up the "...removal of something every day." I've heard answers to this question range from, "I don't know," and, "we've always done this as long as I've been here," to, "that's the way the manager/owner/boss likes to do it." These answers, and those like them, are obstacles to an open conversation about why the task, function, or process is still necessary. The truth is that the current business process owner likely fears that being honest about the process will result in them losing their job. Leaders must face this challenge head on with a view to the good of the entire team and the ability to create sustainable success!

Effective leaders constantly engage in conversations regarding what they need to do more, what they need to start doing, and what they need to stop doing to stay relevant in today's business environment. Tackling the challenge of removal means a leader must ultimately have a clear focus on long-term success and acquiring the knowledge and wisdom to get them there!

What are you removing today to stay relevant?

Lead Well!

Section I: Personal Leadership

There are no time management problems...
there are only priority management problems.

It seems we hear people lament their latest time management problems no matter where we are. Typical fare like, "I didn't have time to..." or, "I ran out of time to..." packs the airwaves with just enough conviction to get us to buy-in to their dilemma and potentially offer some level of sympathy to their plight. Those that know me well will refrain from these statements or catch themselves mid-stream, because they know I will challenge them to restate the truth, "I did not make time to..." The issue here is not about having time because everyone has the same 24 hours to invest, spend, waste, or otherwise use to their choosing. And therein lies the real issue, choosing what to do with our time!

How does a leader make these choices and still keep up with the demands of the 21st Century workplace and family commitments? The secret lies in the ability to prioritize and execute commitments in the order in which they need to be addressed during the 24 hours everyone is given every single day. But let's begin with understanding a few basics about prioritization in order to begin investing time more wisely:

- ✔ **Prioritization means something will not get done today ~** Prioritization, by definition, means saying 'yes' to important tasks and goals. This also means saying 'no' to less important tasks and goals. 'No' is an acceptable answer in business when it is the correct answer for the situation. The secret is in communicating 'no' in a way that explains how and why the priorities are set up the way they are!

- ✔ **Prioritization means there can only be one priority ~** The expression, "If you have ten priorities, then you have no priorities," reflects the trap many leaders get caught in; too many priorities. The long list of seemingly important priorities becomes daunting because leaders either don't take the time to prioritize, don't know how to begin prioritizing, or both. Developing a prioritization method can be as simple as using process of elimination or a more sophisticated team brainstorming discussion. Either way, every successful leader must have a process to determine and effectively communicate priorities to their followers!

- ✔ **Prioritization is a function of goal-planning** ~ When leaders tell me they struggle with time management, the first question I ask is to describe their goal planning process to me. As you might imagine, I get quite a variety of answers from, "I have no goals," To, "I don't bother with goals because they keep changing anyway." It is the plight of many a leader whose goals succums to the supplier chirping the loudest, the customer complaining the most, or, worse yet, the leader's own health screaming for priority (see "First, secure your mask…and then assist the other person."). Well executed goals help the leader best understand where to invest their time.

Sustainable leadership requires effective prioritization to stay abreast of the fluidity of the 21st Century workplace. Having a process that is exercised and communicated regularly can spell the difference between being the leader everyone follows or the leader no one knows how to follow.

How well is your prioritization process working, and how do you know?

Lead Well!

Section I: Personal Leadership

Never stop learning...
because life never stops teaching.

How do leaders stay relevant in today's dynamic economic and political environment? What was relevant five years ago is passé today just like what is relevant today will be on its way to obsolescence three years from now, yet many leaders seem to believe they can stay relevant with skills, knowledge, and attitudes learned years ago. They lament the need for different outcomes for their business (for profit or non-profit) but spend little time actively engaging in the process of staying relevant, the process of continuous learning! Let's break down each of the key areas of learning with some ideas about how to stay relevant in each one.

- ✔ **Learning Relevant Skills** ~ Skills are the things you need to know how to do to be an effective leader. Goal Planning, Effective Communications, and Time/Priority Management are just a few of the key leadership skills required to be an effective 21st Century leader. So, how do you keep these skills relevant? Recognizing what you don't know how to do is the first step in the process of learning. Assessing current skills is important to understand where skill gaps may be. For instance, most leaders recognize the importance of goal planning yet cannot describe their goal planning process. Many leaders recognize the importance of effective listening yet have never learned how to listen well. Objectively assess your skills against the need to be an effective leader and fill in the gaps!

- ✔ **Learning Relevant Knowledge** ~ Knowledge is knowing when and where to appropriately use the relevant skills you have for effective leadership. Knowing when and where to ask the right questions, when and where to delegate or do yourself, and balancing the planning role vs. the controlling role are just a few examples of the leadership knowledge of an effective 21st Century leader. Because knowledge is also information in context, the only way to learn is to consciously put yourself in new situations to exercise your ability to leverage new knowledge. There is an expression that, "learning by definition, will always feel unauthentic." This is absolutely true when leveraging new skills in new situations and context to create new relevant knowledge. Consciously, and proactively, put yourself out of your comfort zone to learn and embrace new leadership knowledge!

✔ **Learning Relevant Attitudes** ~Attitude is the desire, the want, to achieve success as an effective 21st Century leader. It is also habit of thought that must be developed beyond traditional training realms. Once you find the opportunities to step out of your comfort zone and leverage new skills in a new context, the initial experience will be awkward. Creating a new relevant attitude means replacing old habits of thinking with new habits of thinking through repetition. Being accountable to developing these new attitudes will push you past the initial awkwardness to a point where the new skills and knowledge come naturally and require less conscious thought. Use accountability and repetition to consciously and subconsciously develop new leadership attitudes!

Learning new relevant skills, knowledge, and attitudes is continuous process. The reality is that once you've mastered a new set of skills, knowledge, and attitudes, life will present even more new learning opportunities. I had the recent pleasure of listening to Leo Brubaker, Chief Operating Officer of Centro, which grew to a $400M company in 10 years, speak at a Young Professionals recognition event. Several times during his presentation, he spoke directly of needing to "learn how to make money" and "learn how to run a business" over the course of his tenure with the company. As a young professional (under 40 years old) he understands, as all effective leaders do, the importance of continuous learning to making leadership a way of life!

What are you learning today to keep your leadership relevant for tomorrow?

Lead Well!

Section I: Personal Leadership

It's OK to not know how...
It's not OK to avoid learning how!

It's not a secret that continuous learning is an important element of staying relevant in today's business environment. While there are a multitude of reasons and business drivers why this is our reality (technology, global enterprise, socio-cultural shifts to name but a few), it still amazes me how often ignorance is used as an excuse for not keeping up with change, to which I usually respond with the opening quote. Eventually, all leaders arrive at a point of "I don't know..." relative to their business. However, leaders must never fall for "...but I'm not going to worry about it" as a means to avoid learning what they need to know.

In my experience, there are two primary reasons leaders fall into the trap of avoiding the right level of personal development necessary to stay relevant. The first is lacking a complete understanding of what they know and how much of it is still relevant. The second is confusing knowledge of how to do something new with knowing how and when to effectively apply it. We will break down each one here.

Leaders who have over a decade of leadership experience under their belt can easily fall prey to this first blind spot. They settle into a mindset that sounds like "It has worked well over the last 5-6 years so why change?" or "I have over (name your number) years doing this so I know what I'm doing." They become blind the changing conditions and environment of their industry putting themselves and their organization at risk of irrelevance!

The best way to avoid this level of blindness is to balance the leadership decision making process with input from clients (voice of the customer) and input from the members of the organization who deal directly with those clients (sales associates, customer service representative, engineers, etc.). This is what I refer to as "Ground-Truth." Knowing what clients are saying in alignment with what the front lines are saying is a great way to be proactive in effectively meeting the needs of the market!

Section I: Personal Leadership

The sorry state of leadership development is attributed to the second blind spot. When leaders believe that merely knowing something new (training) is the end game, they unknowingly sabotage their own development efforts. It is not what leaders know, it is how they apply what they know that keeps leaders relevant in their industries and markets. I would go so far as to suggest the content (how & what) of effective leadership has not changed much in the last 50 years. However, the context (when & how) of effective leadership changes weekly (daily in some cases)! Effective leaders learn from how they apply what they know and how they exercise this applied learning on a continuous basis. They proactively address the constantly changing definition of what is relevant head-on in order to stay ahead of change!

It is said that learning, by definition, will always feel inauthentic. This means leaders will be uncomfortable in times where they don't know the answer. Avoiding the discomfort of what they don't know is not OK. Taking the right approach to continuous leadership development ensures the leader AND their teams enjoy sustainable success!

How are you truly developing your leadership relevance?

Lead Well!

Section I: Personal Leadership

"Adapt...
or Die"

I was recently reintroduced to Lt. Gen. Rick Lynch's book by the same name as the title. I have always liked the bluntness of the message, especially as it applies to Organizational Culture. The importance of the value and impact of culture begins with understanding what culture really is and that it has multiple moving parts. Once we define what culture is, we can then look at how culture affects organization execution externally as well as how culture impacts organizational operations internally. As leaders continue to fully grasp the nuances of 21st Century Leadership with all its changes, one truth remains constant; Culture will ultimately determine whether success is fleeting or sustainable!

Culture is defined as the system of shared values, beliefs, attitudes and behaviors that develops within an organization and guides the behavior of the members. Culture exists on some level with or without leadership doing anything at all to influence it. It is said the culture of an organization is defined by the time the 20th member is hired. The real issue, then, is whether the culture of the organization, whether for-profit, non-profit, private, public, large or small, is an asset or a liability to the Vision and the Strategy of that organization. How does the culture enable the right behavior of its members to execute its goals in a way that creates sustainable success while at the same time helping members deal with the day-to-day issues of working together?

✔ **Internal Integration** ~ the internal integration dimension of organizational culture deals with how the members create and nurture their own unique identity. When members of an organization spend most of their working weeks together, an identity appears through the hundreds of daily dialogs and interactions the members participate in. These interactions are the basis of judgements by each member that lead to their own characterization of the organizational culture. It may be different for different groups within the organization. The sales team may have a different culture than the human resources team while the marketing team and IT team may not recognize each other's cultures due to their own unique characterizations. However, all these characterizations must align to the overall organizational culture to achieve sustainable success. As Simon Sinek once said, "Customers will never love a company until the employees love it first." Thus, it is crucial the internal integration is in alignment so the external adaptation can succeed.

- ✔ **External Adaptation ~** the external adaptation dimension of organizational culture deals with how the members get things done. It speaks to the mission, strategy and associated goals the members are engaged to achieve and how they achieve them. As members interact, they form deeper understanding of how they contribute to the mission. They may see themselves as valuable knowledge workers to the mission or they may see themselves as expendable and interchangeable resources with only a cost value to the organization. Either way, the culture will unfold as members are able to tell external stakeholders how good they are and support it through the actions members take. The real question remains as to whether the organizational culture supports achieving the desired results for sustainable success!

The ability of a culture to adapt to constant changes in the business environment is crucial to an organization's success. I would go so far as to say that the culture itself is defined as a one of adaptability as its primary characteristic. Having done this in previous organizations I've led, the ability to adjust to environmental changes was paramount to our ability to continue growing despite recessions, industry meltdowns, merger threats and terrorist attacks. All because we knew we had to adapt…or die!

How would you characterize your culture and how is it contributing to sustainable success?

Lead Well!

Section I: Personal Leadership

"A mind that knows how to think is more empowered...
than a mind that only knows what to think."

There have been many times I have witnessed situations with businesses and found myself contemplating, "What were they thinking?" As it turns out, after coming across Neil deGrasse Tyson's words in the title of this article, I was asking the wrong question. I should have asked, "How were they thinking?" as I now believe that answer has greater ramifications in our leadership-challenged world of today! Let's break down his words further to see what we can learn relative to 21st Century leadership.

- ✓ **Only knowing what to think** ~ If we define thinking as "... concentrating on one thing long enough to develop an idea about it," as William Deresiewicz does in his October 2009 lecture to the plebe (freshman) class at the United States Military Academy at West Point, then we can begin to break down the challenges of only knowing what to think. Only knowing what to think implies a lack of original ideas on the part of the leader. The resulting behavior becomes very unoriginal and, in many cases, harmful to the sustainable growth of the team, organization, or business. While it is a short-term safe bet to think like your manager, the long-term results are a culture of groupthink and yes-men/women!

- ✓ **Knowing how to think** ~ It is a long-held contention of mine that the basics of effective leadership have not changed in the last hundred years. Respect, effective communications, trust, teamwork, and a host of other qualities are still as applicable as they were a century ago. What has changed dramatically is how these principles are applied and the speed at which they are applied in the context of 21st Century leadership. Knowing how to focus on something long enough to ponder it from multiple angles and create your own ideas about it is crucial to understanding the right context in any given moment in time. But that takes precious time to do. Those who do it well make the time to reflect and ask themselves, "How does this affect my team, organization, business, and/or customer?" in a meaningful and focused way. Like any learned skill, which knowing how to think is, practice and repetition are required so that it becomes second nature to one's leadership attitude!

✓ **Empowerment for knowing how to think** ~ There are multiple examples in my own career where I can point to my ability to think about a new situation and generate my own ideas about that situation given all the variables. Examples from the military that generated successful missions. Examples from corporate leadership situations where careers, reputations, and, in some cases, lives were on the line. Examples from the classroom where students learned their own version of how to think and not just repeat what someone else told them to think. In every case, I was at least a step ahead of most others because they were thinking the way they had been taught to think which was not as relevant as my own real-time, in-context, new thinking about the situation. Forcing myself to ask questions like "What if…?" and "Why not…?" gave me the insights to be empowered to make leadership decisions that were foreign to others around me!

If you've read this far, you may find yourself asking if you really know how to think or if most of what you think about is what others have told you or taught you to think about. We live in an information-rich, knowledge-poor world. Those who only know what to think have much information to share. Those who know how to think know when and where to share information that matters in the present context, creating knowledge for sustainable success as 21st Century leaders!

How do you think?

Lead Well!

Section I: Personal Leadership

"Are you playing to win...
or playing not to lose?"

This is a question I ask all my clients at one point or another during our time working together. Whether they are a corporate leader over a business unit or division, a non-profit leader of an agency or association, an entrepreneur or small business owner, or even a high school student leader, the intent of the question is always the same. Are they embracing risk or are they avoiding failure? Are they focused on the future or are they leaning too heavily on the past? The question usually comes up as the leader is struggling on some level to lead at the speed of business!

In my own experience working with leaders at all levels described above, there are five keys to success when leading oneself/a team/ an organization in 21st Century business. Collectively, these keys to success support a leadership mindset focused on setting relevant goals and achieving the desired results for sustainable success. They are:

- ✔ **Get Ready to Warp** ~ It is not so much the leader's ability to adapt that matters as much as the speed in which the leader is able to adapt in order to stay relevant. We cannot slow time, so the leader must learn to think faster to remain closer to the forefront of their respective industry!

- ✔ **Servant Leadership** ~ The leader can only be as successful as the team they lead. Anything other than this philosophy towards the team and the leader begins the slow slide into irrelevance!

- ✔ **Cognitive Diversity** ~ Relevant leadership lies in the leader's attitude towards adaptive thinking. Success is in the diverse thinking of the team rather than diverse demographics. A team that thinks differently will ultimately do differently!

- ✔ **Context, not Content** ~ We operate in an information-rich, knowledge-poor business environment. How leaders apply their information to create knowledge-based decisions is more important than the sum total of the information they've accumulated!

Section I: Personal Leadership

✓ **Adaptive Culture** ~ Sustainable success can only occur when the organization embraces adaptability as a cultural norm. The leader cannot possibly have all the answers to change, so creating a culture promoting ideas throughout the organization is paramount to sustainable success!

Each of these five keys to success are necessary to adapt at the speed of business and then some. Business is neither slowing down nor standing pat. It is accelerating as technology approaches the point of singularity, raising the stakes even higher to play to win!

How are you playing to win as a 21st Century leader?

Lead Well!

Section I: Personal Leadership

We are great at goal setting...
we suck at goal achieving!

Full disclosure, I am a goals geek! I've used goals most of my life, beginning at age 12 when I set my first 2 significant goals. The first was to join the Boy Scouts and become an Eagle Scout, which I did 2 years later. The second was to graduate from the United States Military Academy at West Point, which I did 10 years later. To this day, goals continue to play a significant role in our ongoing success at RPC Leadership Associates, Inc. Let's take a deeper look through the research of Edwin Locke and Gary Latham at the five ways goals have high motivational impact.

- ✔ **Challenging Goals are more likely to lead to higher performance** ~ We never really know what we are capable of until we push ourselves, or are pushed by others, to the perceived outer limits of our comfort zone. Of course, challenging goals may not deliver desired results on the first attempt. Goals were never meant to be linear, as life isn't that cooperative. However, even if the path changes, the end goal doesn't have to. If I were to go back to every goal not achieved on the first attempt, I can still articulate what was learned from each situation that helped to ultimately achieve the desired result!

- ✔ **Specific Goals are more likely to lead to higher performance** ~ When working with clients on goal-planning, we always spend time understanding the difference between tangible and intangible goals. "I want to be a better leader" is a statement I hear a lot in my profession. However, as an intangible goal, we have to make it tangible through several iterations of what it means or what it looks like when one is a better leader. Once a clear picture of success is made specific, achieving the goal becomes almost second nature!

- ✔ **Feedback motivates towards higher performance** ~ In my many years as a leader, I've come to realize the only people who don't like feedback on their goals are poor performers. Humans inherently want feedback to know how they are tracking to their desired results. Leaders sometimes fail to realize this and only step in with feedback when the goals are not met. Providing balanced feedback is a crucial leadership skill, especially in a 21st Century workforce!

- ✓ **Goals lead to higher performance when people feel they are capable of achieving them** ~ One of the common mistakes I've seen leaders make is shifting the business strategy without ensuring the existing workforce has the skills needed to achieve the new goals. Change management is a constant leadership challenge so ensuring the team stays relevant with their skills, knowledge, and attitudes gives them the confidence to achieve the desired result!

- ✓ **Goals lead to higher performance when they are accepted and committed to** ~ One of the challenges leaders have to face is getting their team, who likely had little or no input on the goals, to commit to them. There are always benefits to individuals as they achieve goals from higher management. When leaders help their team members see those benefits, they are much more likely to get full commitment. Of course, it does assume the leader knows what each of their team members are striving toward. Achieving alignment between the goals of the organization and individual goals is pure magic!

For these reasons, we do not refer to goal setting, but rather we speak of goal planning as the process to achieve goals. Being effective and successful leaders is not what we intend to do. It is about the desired results we actually achieve to move the team/organization/business forward to enjoy sustainable success!

What desired results did you achieve this year and what did you learn in the process?

Lead Well!

Section I: Personal Leadership

Are we too soft…
on our soft skills?

Much is said and written these days about soft skills and how important they are to business success. Often, the context of this discussion is the evolving influence of technology in our daily lives. Artificial Intelligence (AI), Augmented Reality (AR), and any other technology that threatens (real or imagined) to replace humans in the workforce is a driving force behind the need and effectiveness of our soft skills. It's as if we are less afraid of losing our hard skills and more afraid of our lack of soft skills and ability to think critically!

Let's consider "skills gaps." The November 2018 LinkedIn Workforce Report found the biggest "skills gap" is in San Francisco/Silicon Valley followed by New York City. The top 3 skills gaps in San Francisco/Silicon Valley were Oral Communication, Business Management, and Leadership, in that order. In New York City, the top 3 skills gaps were Oral Communication, Leadership, and Digital Literacy, in that order. So now we have a scenario in which the mecca of digital communications and the most populated city in the country can't find enough people who can carry on a live conversation! What the hell!

I had the opportunity recently to interview a young (mid-twenties) candidate for a client. The conversation led to describing an opportunity to fundraise in his previous role, something he stated he did quite well, compared to his peers. When asked what his secret was, he replied that most everyone else attempted to reach out to donors via email, text, or social media where he had live conversations which generated much higher results. People do business with people they trust, and trust is rarely achieved without some level of live interaction!

What these two examples, as well as the hundreds more I could personally document, tell us is the critical importance of the ability to communicate live and in person is a critical soft skill which a vast majority of the workforce is ignoring.

Section I: Personal Leadership

Leadership is all about soft skills like effective communications (speaking AND listening), emotional intelligence, collaboration, managing change, time management, and critical thinking, just to name a few. Ask yourself, as you make time to set your goals for the new year or the next cycle, what amount of time and resources are you budgeting to strengthen your soft skills? Based on current trends, if it is not more than your investment in hard skills, you are likely falling behind!

How are your soft skills helping you achieve your goals?

Lead Well!!

Section 2:

Leadership Relationships

"No man will make a great leader who wants to do it all himself or get all the credit for doing it." ~ Andrew Carnegie

Once we have a heightened sense of self-awareness, we can effectively lead others. Effective leaders know the importance of establishing and nurturing relationships with their most precious assets: their people! Collaboration is a crucial tool for successful lifelong leaders!

Section 2: Leadership Relationships

"The single biggest problem in communication…
is the illusion that it has taken place."

In the fast-moving, technology-fueled world in which we live and work, we could easily be forgiven for falling prey to the illusion portrayed in George Bernard Shaw's quote above. Shaw, an Irish playwright, won the Nobel Prize for Literature in 1925, so he certainly knew a thing or two about communications. It also supports my belief that there are time-tested tenets of Leadership Communications that are consistent with the passing of time. However, in the modern 24/7 always-on world, the context of Leadership Communications has changed dramatically, further perpetuating the illusion that it actually takes place at all!

Effective leadership occurs when both the sender and the receiver understand the shared meaning of the communication. The illusion comes into play when the meaning is not shared, but the sender thinks it is. In my own 30+ years of experience, effective communications has been and continues to be the greatest challenge leaders face in growing their business (regardless of whether they would admit it or not). Furthermore, I can point to three specific situations every leader, whether a corporate, non-profit, or entrepreneurial leader are faced with where effective communications play a crucial role in a successful outcome to the situation.

- ✓ **"Change is inevitable, growth is not"** ~ Change depends on effective communication for successful execution. The leader must communicate what will change as well as the reason for the change in order to achieve the new state of the business. Regardless of the circumstances, all stakeholders must understand the "why" as well as the "what" and the "how" so the desired results of the change are realized.

- ✓ **"Communications is both the cause and the cure of Conflict"** ~ Conflict is another inevitable reality in today's global economy. The many faces of human diversity create natural conflict on a regular basis, giving leaders ample opportunity to communicate effectively with their organizations. Of note is the leader's ability to listen during conflict situations. While listening is a learned skill, not enough leaders actively and consciously practice it. Communicating and listening effectively during conflict allows leaders to stay in a position to manage the conflict without becoming part of the conflict themselves.

✓ **"You can delegate authority, but you cannot delegate responsibility"** ~ Leaders do not succeed by themselves. Even a solo-preneur has to delegate authority for parts of their business to succeed. By clearly communicating the desired outcome of the delegated task and trusting those being delegating to, the leader confidently assumes full responsibility for the outcome. The team also takes pride in being a trusted, integral piece of their overall success.

A friend of mine once shared a comment she made to a member of her team, "I can explain it to you, but I cannot understand it for you." Effective speaking, active listening, communicating intent, and soliciting feedback all contribute to shared understanding and ensure all parties are on the same page.

How well are you communicating, and how do you know it is not an illusion?

Lead Well!

Section 2: Leadership Relationships

"Strive not to be a success...
but to be of value."

In the last three or four months, not a week passed without discussing the topic of value. Whether it was helping a solo-preneur determine the unique value of their business to the market, coaching a sales team to help prospects determine the difference between the value of their needs and wants, or coaching a corporate leader determining their value to their team, the value topic typically begins with a discussion of how to be more successful. It has me reflecting on how we can apply Albert Einstein's words above to 21st Century leadership opportunities. I find value discussions naturally fall into three distinct categories, so let's take a look at each one through the lens of his words.

- ✔ **Value of Self ~** I often ask members of a business team or those who are in career transition this question, "What is your value to the business?" It still surprises me how often the answer is related to their salary, or former salary. However, that response does allow us to dig deeper into what value is as an employee/team member/ individual contributor. Among other things, it includes the value of their ability to make others better simply by being part of the team. How often do we hear stories of people choosing to work for a smaller salary for the opportunity to work with a high-performing team? In most cases, these team members are providing value well beyond their salary. I often use my experiences in the military and those of my sons as yet another example of individuals whose value transcends their salary.

- ✔ **Value to Team ~** As the leader of a team, it is easy to doubt one's value because you are not actually making/delivering/servicing tangible outcomes like the team is doing. I had this experience as a front-line manager of a high-performing team at Sprint. They really did not need me on a day-to-day basis because they were that good! When I assessed my value to the team, I realized my value was in helping each of them individually grow and improve so that we collectively achieved our goals. As their value to the business improved, my own definition of value evolved which it has continued to do based on what I learned from that team over 20 years ago!

Section 2: Leadership Relationships

- ✓ **Value to Clients ~** It is a classic conversation in the world of sales to know what your unique value proposition is, but we tend to forget who defines the value. When a sales person recites their unique value proposition, I always follow-up with, "How do you know?" Is it based on what marketing tells you or because of what your buyers are telling you? This is an important distinction because value is always correctly defined by the buyer/user of the product/delivery/service your business provides. One client may associate a very high value to a service that another client could care less about. Your value to your clients is to know the difference and evolve as your clients evolve.

Value evolves over time making the discussion of value always on! Whether reflecting on your own personal value to your business or the business's value to the stakeholders, it is a discussion we rarely get to determine ourselves, but getting it right is a crucial element to the sustainable success of our business.

What is your value to your business, and how do you know?

Lead Well!

Section 2: Leadership Relationships

"Forget coping...
think adapting"

For all the time and material I've devoted to helping my clients and students manage change, I could not help but note the simplicity and profoundness of the title quote. What makes it even more credible is it is attributed in a recent "People" magazine article to Dame Judith Dench, winner of an Oscar and a Tony Award at age 65! As the character "M" in many of the James Bond film series, she likely knows what she is talking about, so let's break it down further!

- ✔ **Forget Coping ~** Coping is generally defined as a reaction to minimize stress or conflict. It conjures up images of someone trying to deal with an uncomfortable situation and possibly surviving to move on to another day or the next event. In the leadership context, it portrays the leader who is overcome by the events surrounding them as their world peppers them with problems and challenges. To forget coping then, leaders must remove coping as an option to continue operating in a constantly changing business environment. If a leader's first reaction is coping, I would suggest they are playing "not to lose" as a strategy. Coping may keep you from harm's way in the moment, but little to no progress is made overall.

- ✔ **Think Adapting ~** Whether Dame Judith Dench meant it or not, the choice of words to "Think Adapting" versus simply "Adapt" to complete the sentence is telling. Adapting is much more than reacting or minimizing stressors or conflict. Adaptability begins with an attitude of continuous change and getting out ahead of change to avoid being a victim of it. With mindsets fully supporting adaptability, leaders can create and effectively communicate their Vision and Strategy to their teams. Leaders who are thinking adaptability are playing to win as opposed to playing not to lose! They are consciously and, more importantly, subconsciously adapting to the ever-changing business environment around them.

Section 2: Leadership Relationships

It is said that change is inevitable, but growth is not. In Max McKeown's book, *Adaptability*, he speaks of 17 rules of successful adaptability. "Stability is a Dangerous Illusion" is rule 5. The quest for stability becomes, in its own right, unachievable due to the inevitability of change. The difference in growth occurring or not depends on whether the leaders play not to lose or play to win.

How are you thinking about change?

Lead Well!

Section 2: Leadership Relationships

The best teacher...
is your last mistake.

What is your attitude towards failure? I ask this question, or a variation of it, many times when coaching leaders at all levels of an organization. Interestingly enough, I get more absolute answers from front line managers and supervisors and more broadly defined answers from senior management. Said differently, in my experience, those on the front lines see less leeway for failure, to the point of wanting to be stressfully perfect, whereas those farther removed have a different attitude towards failure, one where it is seen a means to learn and grow. I am not suggesting these experiences are scientifically representative, merely what my experiences are with the topic. The question is, why the difference at all?

It's amazing how frequently we hear about the lessons we learned from our mistakes along the pathway of life. Learning how to walk, riding a bike, driving a car, and all the other things that people learn from doing, making mistakes, and doing again until it was a habit. Yet, when it comes to work and the complexities and challenges that come with achieving desired results, those lessons are forgotten and the impetus for perfection becomes the norm.

The leadership challenge is clear. How does the culture or the organization, which leaders are directly responsible for creating and maintaining, treat mistakes or failures? How do the leaders react when they hear of a mistake or failure within their organization? When I was an executive, when I heard of a mistake, my standard practice was threefold:

- ✔ **Fix the problem** ~ When mistakes are made, the first action is always to fix the problem. Trying to blame someone or something when the problem still exists serves no purpose other than to confuse an already confusing situation. Quite often, if the mistake impacts a client, the client may go down this path right away, and it is the leader's responsibility to direct the initial efforts and focus to fixing the problem!

- ✔ **What happened ~** Here is where my personal philosophy differed from many others. The first person I spoke with was not the person that made the mistake. The first person I spoke with was the manager of the person who made the mistake. My assumption was always that the person who made the mistake did not come to work that day to make the mistake. What was incomplete that caused the mistake?

- ✔ **What was learned ~** Obviously, the person who made the mistake will need to understand what they did wrong, and how they will work with their manager to make different decisions the next time the situation arises, which it will. Closing the loop with an active discussion of what new decisions will be made the next time ensures all concerned have a new mental image of better decisions without feeling like their career is over!

In his 2011 TED Talk, General Stanley McKrystal said, "Leaders can let you fail and yet not let you be a failure." Mistakes are a part of the process and yet failure is really only an issue if nothing was learned from the mistake. The only failure is not learning from our mistakes, everything else is the best teacher we can have!

How do your leadership attitudes and behaviors help your team learn from their mistakes?

Lead Well!

Section 2: Leadership Relationships

"Leaders are sentenced...
by their sentences. "

We've long defined "effective communications" as when the sender and the receiver of a message understand it with the same contextual meaning. As leaders, this is a basic, albeit crucial, element of the success as a 21st Century leader. However, as Warren Bennis reminds us in the title quote, there are consequences associated with the words we use and whether or not they convey their intended contextual meaning. This is especially true when we speak. Technological advances notwithstanding, humans are pre-wired to still respond to the spoken word. The spoken word is hundreds of thousands of years old while the written word is still only several hundred years old. Even in a technology-laced world, the spoken word still rules in the world of effective communications.

In my experience, lack of effective communications is the number one reason why leaders are ineffective in leading their organizations and teams. Worse yet, it is also the number one issue they will not admit they have. It is too easy to blame the receiver of the message or not having enough time to deliver the message effectively. Regardless of the excuse, there are three key reasons why a 21st Century leader needs to know how to communicate via the spoken word effectively:

✔ **Communicating Vision ~** It is hardly a secret how important a vision is to the success of an organization or team. The vision represents the aspirations of the collective people in an organization or team and is understood at a very emotional level. When was the last time a memo or email conveyed emotional inspiration as you read it? If your organization's current vision inspires you, you likely heard it communicated in person first before it was printed and displayed where it would be reinforced. Effective leaders speak with emotion to inspire and evoke an emotional response to the vision!

Section 2: Leadership Relationships

- **Communicating Change** ~ A key reason why leaders communicate the vision effectively is to lead the organization through change. Organizational change, by nature, is hard and can be painful based on our inherent need to for stability. It is known that nature cannot exist in a vacuum. When organizations create an information vacuum through silence or vague communications, people naturally fill it in with their own ideas/stories. This is how rumors, gossip, complaining, and dogmatism begin to fill in the blanks. Effective leaders speak with honesty, integrity, and authenticity to help their organization and teams navigate change and follow the new direction!

- **Communicating in Conflict** ~ Change comes with conflict; as long as there are two people left on earth, there will be conflict! Interestingly enough, communication is both the cause and the cure of conflict. Saying the wrong thing the wrong way at the wrong time will invariably cause conflict. Based on the emotional element inherent in conflict, the most common reaction is to avoid it altogether, followed by over-reaction and escalation. Both reactions intensify the conflict creating more damage than if the conflict had been embraced and dealt with through effective communications. Effective leaders speak to both the substantive and the emotional elements of conflict setting an example for how to communicate effectively for team effectiveness!

Mark Twain once said, "The difference between the right word and the almost right word is the difference between lightning and a lightning bug." In this age of always-on technology, leaders who use the right words to effectively communicate their Vision, the next Change, and embrace Conflict are the ones who are creating a culture of sustainable success for their organizations and teams.

What is your followers' verdict on your spoken communications?

Lead Well!

Section 2: Leadership Relationships

Your "yes" means nothing…
if you can't say "no."

It seems the hardest thing to do in business these days is to say 'No' to someone else. We can think of plenty of times we regret saying 'Yes' when we knew damn well it was going to mess up our current priorities, or worse, put us in a position to be less effective than our capabilities. Let me just put it out there now; 'No' is a legitimate response in any business if it is, in fact, the appropriate response for the situation. While most would agree to this fact intellectually, the majority still struggle with actually doing so! Why is that?

As a business leader, part of the art of the profession is making effective, knowledge-based decisions. A crucial ingredient to this decision-making process is listening to insights from those who work for you; including insights that may contrast with your own thoughts on the topic. If your culture is such that it is not safe to disagree, to say 'No' with a platform to state an opposing view, the final decision will be flawed. As the expression goes, "If all you hear from your team is 'Yes', then one of you is redundant." Leaders must be secure enough to let 'No' be an answer just as easily as 'Yes'.

Non-profit leaders struggle with this idea probably more than others, in my experience, due to the very altruistic nature of their industry. Their Mission-centric world is about helping others and saying 'Yes' to every request for help and assistance. Saying 'Yes' and over-committing the organization puts the credibility of the leader at risk. Eventually their 'Yes' loses its meaning as the title suggests. Knowing when to say 'No' for the health of the organization is crucial to its ability to continue to execute its Mission.

Sometimes we have to say 'No' to customers! I am amazed at how often a business owner or business-unit leader will say 'Yes' to a customer out of fear of offending them, knowing full well they just put other customers in jeopardy! Of course, I am not referring to the occasional out-of-the-box request or true crisis that comes along and must be dealt with accordingly. I am speaking to the habit of saying 'Yes' out of fear and/or not knowing how to say 'No' without actually saying the word 'No'!

Section 2: Leadership Relationships

'No' is an appropriate answer as a business leader when the situation calls for it. Learning to say 'No' without using the word 'No' is important because people just don't like hearing the word. For example: When someone interrupts you with, "Have you got a minute?" and you actually do not have time for them right now, respond with "Because I am working on a high-priority project right now, let's schedule some time after 3:00 today." Saying 'No' without using the word 'No'!

Effectively communicating with stakeholders requires a sense of purpose combined with the skills to use appropriate language to convey true intent. Saying 'Yes' to avoid conflict actually makes the conflict worse. Saying 'Yes' to your manager when you actually disagree makes you a party to the slow degradation of the culture. Saying 'Yes' to a customer without clarifying the real need means putting the relationships with that client, as well as other clients and associates, at risk.

Gandhi once said, "A 'No' uttered from the deepest conviction is better than a 'Yes' merely uttered to please, or worse, to avoid trouble." A leader's word is their bond and their brand. If their 'Yes' has no meaning because they can't say 'No', then their brand loses its Value.

How much does your 'Yes' mean?

Lead Well!

Section 2: Leadership Relationships

It's not the facts we disagree on...
it's on the interpretation of the facts we most often disagree!

Within this classic conflict between content (facts) and context (interpretation) lies a key element of effective leadership; managing perceptions! We've heard many of the mantras around perception including the most common, "Perception is Reality." But what is perception and how does it influence our ability to lead effectively? Perception is the process we use to organize and interpret our sensory inputs in order to understand, and give meaning to, what goes on around us. More specifically, perception can be addressed by looking deeper into the factors that shape our perceptions which reside in the Perceiver, the Situation, and the Sensory Target. Let's look at each of these to see what we can learn to be more effective leaders!

- ✔ **The Perceiver** ~ Even before we encounter our next sensory input, our previous experiences and attitudes will impact how we interpret, or simply interact with (see, hear, taste, smell, and feel) the next event. An example comes from my work coaching leaders with a multi-generational workforce. The leader's attitudes towards members of other generations will undoubtedly bias their interpretation of their interactions. This bias comes naturally as a by-product of the leader's previous experiences in similar situations. As Anais Nin once said, "We don't see things as they are. We see them as we are."

- ✔ **The Situation** ~ Where and how the sensory input occurs has influence over the perception as well. In my own coaching experience, an example we see often occurs when people interpret the same situation differently depending on whether the interaction occurs face-to-face versus being online or on the phone. The contextual setting of the situation impacts and influences how we perceive it!

- ✔ **The Sensory Target** ~ Sensory target (person, place, or thing you're interacting with) characteristics have influence over our perception of events. We interpret interactions differently depending on whether the target falls into a specific category or demographic. Because we do not view targets in isolation, we rely on categories and groupings to help us understand situations. An example, again from my own experience, is the aforementioned multi-generational workforce. We perceive someone in their twenties or early thirties as potentially inexperienced (category) due to their age. Yet that same person likely has much to offer in the way of new ideas to help the leader and the organization stay relevant!

Perception is an integral part of a leader's effectiveness and sustained success based on the many interpretations people can create for a single set of facts. One only has to tune into the current political scene to know how true that really is! Leaders must remember that even when the facts suggest a situation has changed, the change may not be perceived for a couple of cycles. How many cycles depends on the leader's ability to manage the perceiver (themselves and others), the situation, and the target, which are all in constant flux. Developing effective perception management goes a long way to making leadership a way of life!

How are your followers interpreting your facts?

Lead Well!

Section 2: Leadership Relationships

Don't tell me...
show me.

We define Integrity as the alignment of what we think, what we say, and what we do so that they all tell the same story. We are constantly judged on how these three dimensions align as we interact with others. However, only two of these are visible to others and influence how others view us. In personal settings, the misalignment between these elements may create some personal conflict. As leaders, the misalignment between our words and our actions could ultimately destroy us!

It is amazing to me how leaders will say they plan on doing one thing and then ultimately do something else without realizing the consequences of that disconnect! For example, a leader says they are committed to the mission and strategy of the organization while they consistently miss meeting goals and delivering on the promise. When it comes time for that leader's manager to evaluate that leader's integrity, they are given an excellent rating. How can that be? If actions do not support words, the leader is clearly out-of-integrity, a term not widely spoken yet more widely displayed. How do leaders maintain their integrity in the complex world that is today's leadership environment?

- ✔ **Out-of-integrity** is real! Not only does it exist, but it has negative consequences ranging from the "white-lie" variety to the complete breakdown of trust in leadership. Integrity is not situational, although leaders will certainly face a plethora of situations that will challenge their integrity on a regular basis. Recognize the condition of out-of-integrity in your beliefs, words, and actions and be clear on what actions you will take to avoid letting it enter your own leadership accountability mindset!

- ✔ **If you say it, do it!** You would think this would be easy enough for any leader. Usually, leaders say things they have every intention of doing. Of course, occasionally we encounter an out and out liar (although I hesitate to put them in the leader category at all). Typically, it is the well-intended leader who realizes there are more obstacles to following through than originally thought. Either that or the original conditions and/or assumptions changed which happens often. In either case, the integrity remains intact through continuous communications, updated for the new conditions. Followers would rather hear the updated narrative than hear nothing from a leader's fear of being wrong!

✓ **If you can't do it, don't say it!** I find this is the most difficult scenario for leaders to grapple with. This requires leaders to have a true assessment of what is and is not possible for both themselves and their organizations. It requires a correct assessment of personal strengths and weaknesses and a public admission (passively or directly) that they do not have all the answers. It requires leaders to have a plan that sets expectations for what and why the organization competes the way it does. Those who know me well know I often state, "Hope is not a strategy," when speaking of knowing your business strategy. Leaders must commit to their plan in both word and action in a way that the organization can accomplish their mission!

When all is said and done, people want to be led well. Leading with integrity where beliefs, words, and actions are in full alignment with each other means expectations are fully understood. Followers base their level of trust on how well what they see aligns with what they hear from their leaders. What the organization sees and hears from its leaders ultimately sets the stage for sustainable success!

What narrative are your words and actions telling your followers?

Lead Well!

Section 2: Leadership Relationships

"No matter how thin the pancake, it always has two sides."

Over the last five years, I presented multiple versions of our popular "Generational Diversity in the Workplace" presentation to dozens of different audiences. While each audience is unique, a common question usually arises along the lines of, "I fit the generational demographics, but I don't think like my generation." Each time, this question, and subsequent conversation, brings me back to the wisdom from my aunt in the title as it frames for me the value of understanding psychographics to be an effective leader in today's dynamic business environment.

Psychographics are qualitative methodologies based on people's attitudes and values. Most of us are used to demographics which are quantitative, tried and true "labels" to help us organize what is going on around us. If we only focused on demographics, the best we could hope to gain would be effective management. However, we don't lead demographics, we lead people who are more truly defined at their core by their attitudes and values. Everyone's behavior is ultimately defined by their attitudes and values, so it is crucial that leaders understand how to leverage them to achieve sustainable success. The following are two specific applications of this idea:

✔ **It's about Cognitive Diversity** ~ The importance of diversity to the growth of an organization is widely known. Unfortunately, most efforts to create or achieve diversity are based on the use of demographics, typically because they are easier to track and manage. But just because people have cultural, gender, or age differences does not automatically mean diversity of thought! Our behavior is a function of our attitudes, which are habits of thought. If we want different results, leaders must inspire different behavior. Different sustainable behavior means team members are ultimately thinking differently, the product of cognitive diversity. Therefore, leaders who can define and inspire an attitude of adaptability through diversity of thought are the ones who will be most effective and successful!

Section 2: Leadership Relationships

- ✔ **Innovation begins with Creativity** ~ The need to continuously adapt to the constant pressures of change will always exist for leaders. These pressures come from the external environment outside the organization (globalization, technology, political and legal, etc.) as well as within the organization itself (integration, growth, identity, etc.). Innovation, by definition, is doing things differently. However, effective leaders know that to do different, they and their team members must think different. Innovation begins with the creativity that comes from cultivating a cognitively diverse team, and sustainable success comes from leaders who insist that it happen as part of their culture!

What we believe, we think and what we think, we do. If leaders want different behaviors, they must have a team that thinks differently. I have enjoyed much success in my military and corporate careers by asking my teams variations of "What if…?" and "Why not…?" Ultimately, I was getting them to think differently about what might be on the other side of the pancake!

What new behavioral action is your leadership thinking enabling?

Lead Well!

Section 2: Leadership Relationships

"If you want to go fast, go alone...
but if you want to go far, go together."

I came across this quote, which is actually an African proverb, in a post from Joe Tzu who I met years ago as an up and coming young leader in our community. I immediately saw the value in this thought process as it relates to the relationships needed to achieve sustainable success as part of a team. It is also a reflection of a challenge I see on leadership teams that are achieving good results. In this "good is the enemy of great" situation, the team represents a group of individuals all going fast, not a team that is willing to go far!

When I coach leadership teams, the conversation invariably leads to trust as an obstacle to truly effective teamwork. This is not a new concept as most every book that talks about teamwork like Five Disfunctions of a Team, The Wisdom of Teams, and Team of Teams, just to name a few from my own bookshelf, speak implicitly to the level of trust within the team. To take the concept further, team trustworthiness is a combination of three variables:

- ✔ **Credibility ~** In order for a team to move together in unison on a base of trust, every leader on the team must be credible. Do the other leaders believe each of their peers will walk the talk and deliver when and how they say they will deliver? Being good to one's word is a basic character building-block of any effective leader!

- ✔ **Reliability ~** Where credibility is built on being able to walk the talk, reliability means leaders will walk the talk consistently. Can the team count on each leader to consistently be there when they are needed to carry their load of the total leadership burden? Doing well once is a start. Doing well consistently is what will take the team far!

Section 2: Leadership Relationships

- ✔ **Intimacy ~** The distance a leadership team can go will be based on how safe they feel with each other in the heat of battle. It doesn't have to be military battle, just any situation where there is conflict, disagreement, or disruption in the plan where emotions can become a factor, positively or negatively. Do leaders feel they can communicate directly and openly with each other without the concern of judgement, backbiting, or other political shenanigans that might not get in the way of going fast, but will certainly get in the way of going far?

Leadership is setting goals and achieving desired results over and over again. Sustainable success is the only way leaders stay in the game, and they rarely, if ever, achieve that level of success as a solo act. Trusting peer leaders is paramount to sustainable success!

How far are you going with your current level of trust?

Lead Well!

Section 2: Leadership Relationships

To learn you have to listen...
to improve you have to try.

In nearly all of my coaching engagements, speeches, and workshops, the question of value, which I also use synonymously with relevance, comes up in the discussion. It is an issue all leaders grapple with and is complex in that it means something different to just about everyone! So, what does creating sustainable value entail in order to create desired results?

- ✔ **To learn you have to listen** ~ Whenever I do sales-related coaching, we spend time early in the discussion with the concept of helping others buy rather than selling to them. This requires effective listening to understand what is valuable to the prospect or client. In similar fashion, leaders of teams must listen effectively for the same reason. Creating sustainable value requires a level of listening that generates trust between leader and team and allows the leader to truly learn the value of the team and leverage it to achieve the desired results!

- ✔ **Think differently to do differently** ~ It is fair to say that staying relevant over time requires new attitudes and mindset around what value means now versus what it meant last year or five years ago. If the listening described above is filtered through old thinking, the context needed to generate new value will be lost. Effective leaders read regularly and are continuously learning. They have a built-in learning process that allows them to embrace and model new thinking for their team. Creating new value begins with new attitudes that transcend any previous definition and always requires change!

Section 2: Leadership Relationships

- ✔ **To improve you have to act** ~ I took some literary license with the original version of the title quote by Thomas Jefferson. Creating sustainable success and relevance requires conscious action to create new value. Unfortunately, this need to act always bumps up against the past and generates resistance to change, especially if the previous definition of value still lingers in the organization. The intent to act is not enough in today's dynamic business environment. Many of my own clients have heard me ask, when they talk about trying to do something new, "How do we take 'try' out of your last statement?" It is crucial that value is actually realized through deliberate action toward creating sustainable success!

Staying relevant means the definition of value evolves and changes over time. In many cases, this change can happen at a pace that challenges even the most effective leaders. But those leaders know that the future will belong to the leaders who create change today because a successful tomorrow demands it!

How is your leadership creating sustainable value for your organization and how do you know?

Lead Well!

Section 2: Leadership Relationships

The absence of conflict...
does not equal the presence of trust.

Five years ago, I wrote these words in a blog detailing the important elements of trust. They recently came back to me as the topic surfaced in many coaching conversations over the last several months. There was a leader struggling to verbalize the diminished trust they had with a key associate and a leadership team concerned that a public proclamation of trust as a value would somehow have a negative effect (think images of the sleazy salesperson who leads with "trust me" accompanied by a sly grin!). These, and other similar conversations, have me wondering why something so obviously key to effective leadership would be so difficult to verbalize. Upon reflection, I found the conversation broke down into two primary categories of trust: Ethics and Compliance.

- ✔ **Trust based on Ethics ~** Trust based on ethics suggests leaders and followers trust each other to do the right things at the right times simply because they believe it is right! It stems from the beliefs, attitudes, and norms that motivate members of the organization to do what is right whether or not anyone is watching. I often refer to this environment as 'playing to win' by getting things done and done the right way!

- ✔ **Trust based on Compliance ~** Trust based on compliance suggests leaders and followers trust each other to do the right things at the right times because those are the rules! It stems from rules and legal procedures that motivate members of the organization based on an element of fear and the need to avoid negative consequences of breaking the rules. I refer to this environment as one of playing 'not to lose' as the focus is less about advancing the organization than it is about survival of the individual leader or follower.

Section 2: Leadership Relationships

Whether leaders and followers trust based on ethics or compliance, the underlying foundation for both is the organization's culture. As we define culture as the combined beliefs, values, attitudes, behaviors, and norms that guide the actions of the organization, we can easily see how important it is to trust. Does trust come naturally based on a culture that engenders authentic collaboration between leaders and followers? Or is trust forced and guarded based on a culture that focuses on rule-following and blame between leaders and followers?

Going back to the title, just because there is no conflict does not mean that trust exists between leaders and followers. In fact, a sound argument can be made that the presence of conflict is, in and by itself, a sign that leaders and followers trust each other well enough to disagree in pursuit of the best decisions for the organization!

What is the trust in your organization based on, and how do you know?

Lead Well!

Section 2: Leadership Relationships

Strength lies in differences...
not in similarities.

Successfully leading at the speed of business is rooted in diverse thinking. People who think different, will ultimately do different and will be more comfortable with change and adapting at the speed of business! What does Cognitive Diversity entail and what do leaders need to know to leverage the strengths that Stephen Covey alludes to in the title to achieve effective and successful leadership?

- ✓ **Key in on Psychographics vs. Demographics** ~ Most of us are familiar with demographics that look at population groups based on age, income, race, religion, and zip codes, to name but a few. But just because a group looks different, doesn't mean they think different. Psychographics look at the population through the lens of attitudes, aspirations, and other psychological criteria. This information provides leaders the ability to act on how people think with the understanding that how people think ultimately drives how people act!

- ✓ **Embrace Creativity** ~ Much has been written about the role of innovation in adapting at the speed of business. However, innovation doesn't just happen because leaders want it to. What gets less press is the role of creativity in the innovation process. Where innovation is 'doing differently,' creativity is 'thinking differently' and is the foundation for innovation. Creative people are constantly challenging the norm through "What if" or "Why not" responses. Creative people might also be characterized as curious and even artistic but always in the context of achieving desired results for the organization!

Section 2: Leadership Relationships

✔ **Understanding What We Think, We Do** ~ Leading at the speed of business means adapting faster than the competition in a way that achieves desired results. When leaders need different results, their teams and organizations must act different lest things fall prey to the colloquial definition of insanity (doing the same thing over and over expecting different results!). We know that external efforts to change behavior, rewards, and/or fear have temporary impacts over time. The only way a leader and their team can act different is to think different about what they do, why they do it, and how they do what they do. Reframing how the organization's leaders think about the competition can open new avenues of thought and adaptability in a constantly changing business environment!

Effective adaptability is a mindset before it becomes a behavior. Leading at the speed of business requires a constant look at adaptability to stay relevant beyond the drifts in markets and competition. Leaders, and the teams they lead, must all embrace an attitude of change and adaptability in order to take the right actions for sustainable success. In the words of Mary Engelbreit, "If you don't like something, change it; If you can't change it, change the way you think about it."

How are you finding strengths in differences on your team?

Lead Well!

Section 2: Leadership Relationships

You never get a second chance...
to make a good first impression.

As leaders, we have countless opportunities to make good first impressions no matter the industry, market, or business model. This is especially true in today's dynamic business world in and amongst all the clutter of so many "impressions" we come across on a daily basis where relationships ultimately carry the day.

There is one facet of making a good first impression that I see organizations, large and small, for-profit and non-profit, public and private, struggle with: creating and executing an effective onboarding process. I maintain there is very little else that says an organization cares about a person's success in their new role than an effective onboarding process! My focus here is not to define the perfect onboarding process, as that should be organization specific. My focus, instead, is to share some thoughts on effective onboarding at three different levels of the organization; Entry Level, Front-line Manager Level, and Executive Level. Each level has unique aspects to it, yet all have the same purpose: to make a great first impression by setting the person up for success from day one!

- ✔ **Entry Level** ~ This is likely the most important onboarding process for any organization. The new hire is new to the job, new to the organization, and, quite possibly, new to the industry. What is the new person's impression of the organization going to be based on? Are they being thrown into the fray immediately to sink or swim, or are they eased into the role so they can build on small successes along the way? If we know that most people quit their manager, not their job, what is the entry level person's manager's role in the process? How does the person's new team factor into the process? While there are clearly a multitude of HR, IT, and other related tasks that need to be completed, my experience suggests the new person's leader has the most important role in the overall success of this onboarding process!

Section 2: Leadership Relationships

- **Front-line Manager Level** ~ There is no greater personnel decision an organization makes than who they put on their leadership team! This person now has influence over themselves as well as every person on their new team. Has this new manager been set up for some level of leadership development as they move from worker to supervisor? Is this new manager's manager dedicating enough time to ensure they are effectively grounded in their new responsibilities? Any time I had a new manager come on board, I would immediately let the rest of the team know I would not be as accessible to them as I was devoting a lion's share of my time to the new manager during their first 90 days. It is still astounding to me how many organizations fail to recognize the difference between super-worker and super-visor by not effectively transitioning the new manager physically and mentally to the new role!

- **Executive Level** ~ Some may ask why an onboarding process is even necessary for an executive with all the experience they bring to the role, especially if they are promoted from within the organization. Leading as an executive is very different from leading as a manager in the scope and scale of responsibilities. Success is now achieved through other management levels as opposed to by the manager's direct influence on the front-line associates. At this level, it is important to put listening as a key element of the onboarding process. Who are the key people on the team (management and non-management)? What are the strengths and/or blind spots of the existing leadership team? What are the key processes and tools needed to be effective as a team? How many of these processes are documented and do they still work? Achieving sustainable success through others is understanding the answers to these and other key questions to get the executive off on the right foot!

Section 2: Leadership Relationships

As a new employee and a new manager, my own personal onboarding experiences left much to be desired. I was left to figure out how to navigate the organization, the technology, and the processes on the backs of anyone who would answer my questions, usually after I did something unknowingly wrong. As a new manager, I received little to no guidance from my management team and relied heavily on previous military leadership experience. Fortunately, my entry into the executive ranks was much more positive. I had regular meetings with other executives and was given the time to conduct an effective listening tour. It set the stage for many years of effective executive leadership across three different companies!

These experiences are also personal reminders of the importance of onboarding as we work with leaders, either reactively or proactively, who are looking to make a great first impression or are looking for the second chance to make a great second impression!

What was the first impression created by your onboarding process?

Lead Well!

Section 2: Leadership Relationships

Prospects are highly informed...
but not necessarily accurately informed.

With the amount of information leaders have access to increasing at an alarming rate, it comes as is no surprise that leaders find it difficult to be accurately informed enough to make the decisions needed to keep the team, agency, or business growing.

It's been said people don't typically disagree on the facts, rather people typically disagree on the interpretation of the facts. As the pace of change increases, so, too, does the pressure to make decisions in less time to keep up with change. Clearly, context matters in any crucial conversation, and, of course, context takes time to create and communicate. Leaders often argue that they do not have time to create effective context. My push back is always that leaders cannot afford not to create context for their teams. When we play out the consequences of content-only decisions with teams executing out of context, we find that it takes three to five times more time to course-correct or restart the execution. If even a fraction of that time had been applied to creating meaning and understanding (context), the team would be well ahead in executing their operations. As the saying goes, "We don't have time to do it right, but we always have time to do it again!"

We receive a steady diet of news nuggets, sound-bites, and tweets on a daily basis. In the context of this discussion (see what I did there!), this presents the challenge of "availability bias." Availability bias occurs when we assume events are more common than they are based on one or two examples. In a 10/24/18 article in the USA Today titled Smile – things aren't as bad as your brain thinks they are., Jeff Stibel explains how, factually, we are so much better off than we were 50 years ago, yet the general perception is the opposite. Leaders have a responsibility and a challenge to fight through these biased perceptions and bring the facts (content) of the issue to bear as well as the meaning of the facts (context) to make the right decision!

Section 3: Organizational Leadership

"Information is knowing tomato is a fruit. Knowledge is knowing not to put it in a fruit salad." Applying meaning and context to an abundance of facts is critical to the sustainable success of every organization. It falls on the shoulders of organizational leaders to ensure their teams/agencies/businesses understand why their next actions are important to their growth strategies!

How are you ensuring you have accurate facts before making your next key decision?

Lead Well!

Section 2: Leadership Relationships

To win in the marketplace…
you must first win in the workplace!

Whether leading a growing small business, an established large business, or a non-profit enterprise, staying relevant will always be a concern. Establishing, maintaining, and encouraging a culture that views adaptability as a norm rather than something members of the organization have to do is imperative to staying relevant in today's business environment. Culture is who they are, not just what they do. Adaptability is how the organization collectively thinks in order to achieve sustainable success!

It is always important to level-set definitions with the audience so discussions don't get side-tracked. We define culture as the shared set of beliefs, values, attitudes, behaviors, and norms within an organization that guide the actions of its members. Every organization, large or small, private or public, for-profit or non-profit, has a culture based on that definition. The question for organizational leaders is, "Is it the culture we need to achieve sustainable success?" Doug Conant's quote in the title sums up the importance of workplace culture as a means to success in the marketplace. To create and nurture an adaptable culture, here are a few key themes from my own experiences that must be considered:

- ✔ **Engagement from the bottom up** ~ A predominantly top-down culture (where most of the new ideas come from senior management) can certainly achieve some level of adaptability as long as senior leaders are actively engaged. The reality is that truly adaptable cultures trust and expect new ideas from the people who actually work with clients and generate the revenue that drives the business. I've always called this the search for "ground truth" which is a version of what's really happening that leaders cannot get from reading reports. This concept also greatly depends on whether the frontline organization trusts their senior leadership enough to bring fresh ideas based on what they see day-in and day-out. It doesn't mean every idea is one that will be executed, but every idea from the organization must be acknowledged!

Section 2: Leadership Relationships

- ✓ **Consistent Culture Definition** ~ "Tell me about the culture of your organization," is one of my favorite inquiries for a leader I've just met.. I get a variety of answers ranging from a blank stare/silence to a five-minute ramble in hopes they say something that resembles a good answer. In between are answers that not only clearly demonstrate an understanding of the culture but also how they contribute and fit within the stated culture. If a leader and their team either can't define or have widely different ideas around the organizational culture, staying relevant in a sustainable way will likely elude them!

- ✓ **Promote Proactive Change** ~ How does the culture actively promote proactive change, and how does the leader know? Staying relevant is not just about reacting to shifting market conditions; those are table stakes in the game of adaptability. It also means taking the risks associated with proactive change. Being the first one to do anything in business is risky by definition. Promoting a culture of experimentation and ongoing pilot programs sends a strong signal to the organization that being proactive and leading from the front are integral to the organizational culture!

Sustainable success can only occur when the organization embraces adaptability as a cultural norm. Business moves too fast to legislate adaptability solely from the top of the organization. In all my corporate executive roles, one of the consistent messages to the organization was, "We need 100% from 100%." It meant that everyone had a voice and any new idea would be acknowledged to help the organization stay relevant!

How are you adapting to win in your workplace?

Lead Well!

Section 3:

Organizational Leadership

"A leader is best when people barely know he exists…when his work is done, his aim fulfilled, they will all say: We did it ourselves." ~ Lao Tzu

No matter how well the organization is stacked individually, the combined efforts must still generate desired results. Successful lifelong leadership is achieved by creating an environment where people can succeed individually AND collectively!

Section 3: Organizational Leadership

"Strategy...
is a series of expedients."

Helmuth Von Moltke was regarded as one of the greatest military strategists of the late 19th Century. In the military context, his statement above meant no battle plan survives contact with the enemy. Strategy becomes one of extensive preparation for all possible outcomes. Flash forward nearly 150 years and business and military leaders alike find themselves in a similar environment where the key success factor is adaptability. It is still about successfully preparing for all possible contingencies they might encounter in their area of engagement.

So what does it take to plan for a series of expedients? In my experience in the military and in business, I've found 3 common elements of successful adaptability:

- ✔ **Know Your Environment** ~ The military continuously updates threat assessments based on changes in enemy activity. Successful businesses routinely update their environmental assessment and SWOT (Strengths, Weaknesses, Opportunities and Threats) Analysis. While in the military, I've operated in environments of 130° F and -100° F. The business environment can change just as dramatically in the current regulatory and competitive global landscape. We do not have the luxury of, "If we only had more time," or, "If we could go back to the way we were," anymore. (I've heard both multiple times in the last 90 days!) We must create processes to understand the environment including early detection of shifting forces!

- ✔ **Identify Potential Obstacles Up-Front** ~ Adaptability suffers when encountering obstacles without a plan to overcome them. Whether looking at personal goals or organizational strategies, identifying potential obstacles up front reflects both an understanding of the environment and an ability to keep an open mind to other options. Once the obstacles are documented (there are always obstacles!), possible solutions can be created to overcome them. While the possibility exists the obstacle might not appear, having a contingency to overcome it is still better than not having a contingency if the obstacle is encountered!

Section 3: Organizational Leadership

- ✓ **Everyone Understands the Mission** ~ Once the battle begins, real-time intelligence becomes the lifeline of the military commander. Business is no different where leaders depend on real-time intelligence from their field operations (sales, engineering, customer service, etc.). Intelligence from the field supports the success of the Strategy only to the extent that the entire organization understands the Mission. When everyone understands the desired results and has effective communications channels, the business leader has a clear picture of what is truly happening!

Adaptability is the ability to change to fit a new set of circumstances. Successful business leaders adapt from a position of knowledge of their environment; the rest react to the environment with less than ideal consequences.

How are you helping your organization adapt?

Lead Well!

Section 3: Organizational Leadership

"A wealth of information creates…
a poverty of attention."

In the January/February 2014 issue of *Psychology Today*, the headline article was about how super-taskers manage to keep their focus in spite of juggling seemingly endless tasks. In light of overwhelming research stating the brain cannot multi-task, these super-taskers make it look easy. In truth, they are not multi-tasking. They have developed an ability to block out the distractions and focus their attention on the important things they have to do. Given that most people in your business do not have this ability, it rests on the leader to help them weed through the noise to focus on what is really important.

As a leader, the best way to ensure everyone in your business effectively blocks out inconsequential information around them is through clear, complete, and concise communication built around a theme of simplicity. We work and live in a complex world. Complexity on its own generates a wealth of information that needs to process through the organization. However, just because information exists, we do not have to consume it. A leader's greatest value, then, is their ability to simplify the core theme to help everyone in their business understand the message in its proper context. This can be done by remembering the three "C"s of effective communications; Clear, Complete, and Concise.

- ✔ **Clear** ~ While it may not be practical to clarify the meaning of every communication within the organization, clarity is imperative when the communication involves messages important to the success of the organizational direction and culture. Too many implied communications will cause recipients to create their own interpretation, many of which will be incorrect.

- ✔ **Complete** ~ It constantly amazes me when leaders leave out parts of crucial communications based on preconceived notions about what the organization should already know. While the assumption may be true, it is better to be complete than wrong. Complete communications ensure everyone in the organization understands the message in the intended context.

Section 3: Organizational Leadership

✔ **Concise** ~ There is nothing more satisfying than listening to a leader who conveys a clear and complete message in as little time as possible. Attention spans are short. The leader must take the time to craft a concise message to the organization. The longer the message, the greater chances are that the takeaways will be unclear. Don't hope everyone paid attention to the end, know the message was concise – yet thorough – enough that the message was received before they had a chance to tune out!

We live and work in an information-rich, knowledge-poor world. Even though the title quote by Herbert Simon is from the 1970s, around-the-clock connectivity makes the issue now even more complex. The 21st Century leader's greatest challenge is communicating clear, complete, and concise expectations to all the stakeholders in a way that empowers them to execute with the same picture of success in their minds.

How are you avoiding the poverty of attention in your business?

Lead Well!

Section 3: Organizational Leadership

The bitterness of poor quality lingers...
long after the sweetness of low price is forgotten.

We've all heard the expression, "Price, Quality, Time ~ Pick One!" We've all heard the expression, "Price, Quality, Time ~ Pick One!" Business leaders face these options frequently as they address the wants and needs of their external and internal stakeholders. When we think of quality, we think of what degree of excellence we are willing to put forth to achieve the goals in front of us. In today's 21st Century business, achieving excellence is a lofty goal as the market expectations continue to raise the bar on what defines excellence. Failure to step up to the evolving definition of quality generally stems from choosing the path of least resistance, settling for "good is good enough," or just plain laziness! As we think about quality from a business leader's point of view, let's explore the three areas of quality that have the most profound impact on achieving sustainable success:

- ✔ **People ~** Yes, quality people must always be a leader's first priority! A key distinction here is how leaders base their definition of quality people. Many may default to those who can get the job done. Unfortunately, just getting the job done is akin to choosing the "lowest price" and living with the bitterness of poor attitudes and minimalist effort in the work. Others may default to those who strive for perfection. Unfortunately, perfection is not achievable and will drive more stress and anxiety in its pursuit than delivering positive long-term results. Hiring and developing people with the right attitudes and skills to deliver excellent results requires the leader to define what excellence means and leading the team to achieve those standards of excellence over and over again!

- ✔ **Processes ~** Most leaders spend their time managing quality in the area of processes, and for good reason. It is estimated that up to 94% of issues in organizations are process-related as opposed to people-related. Ancillary to that statistic is that poor processes will ultimately ruin good people, so it stands to reason that once the leader has hired the right people, developing quality processes should quickly follow to support the team. In this case, the impact of quality process improvement is to reduce all waste in the process and/or increase the speed of the process, both of which have real financial impact!

- ✔ **Tools and Technology ~** When the right people are on board and the core and supporting processes are fully documented with means to keep them relevant, achieving sustainable success will still depend on the quality of the tools leveraged to execute the processes. It is not simply a matter of automating the current processes. I've seen many business leaders make a key mistake by spending time and money deploying tools that other organizations use or are widely popularized in the business press when their business would have benefited more from just improving processes (which usually costs less time and money!). Taking a process that is half-baked and/or undocumented and applying automation to it merely means the poor results will be achieved faster! Quality tools are those that have real, measurable value to the goals of the business and leverage the full value of the people and processes that use them!

In addition to providing key linchpins between effective strategy and achieving desired results, these three areas must be taken in the order they are listed above. When organizations deploy technology that dictates a process at the expense of people, the process backfires on itself and more damage is done than good. When quality people leverage quality processes with quality tools, the value is not only measurable, it is on a scale more valuable to sustainable success

What does poor quality taste like in your business?

Lead Well!

Section 3: Organizational Leadership

We live in an Information-rich...
Knowledge-poor world.

In 2010, the Institute For The Future (IFTF) published a report titled *Future Work Skills 2020*. The report outlined six key drivers of change over the following ten years as well as ten skills required by the future workforce to meet those disruptive drivers of change. Of course, it is not only the future workforce that needs to develop these future skills. The future leadership structure, which enables the workforce to optimize these skills, will also need to adapt to the new reality. While 2010 seems an eternity ago, the key points of their future predictions are now our present reality!

According to the IFTF, the six descriptive drivers of change are Extreme Longevity, Rise of Smart Machines and Systems, Computational World, New Media Ecology, Superstructured Organizations, and Globally Connected World. In order to adapt to these disruptive forces, the ten skills for success identified by IFTF are:

- ✔ **Sense Making** ~ ability to determine the deeper meaning or significance of what is being expressed.

- ✔ **Social Intelligence** ~ ability to connect to others in a deep and direct way, to sense and stimulate reactions and desired interactions.

- ✔ **Novel and Adaptive Thinking** ~ proficiency at thinking and coming up with solutions and responses beyond which is rote and rules-based.

- ✔ **Cross-Cultural Competency** ~ ability to operate in different cultural settings.

- ✔ **Computational Thinking** ~ ability to translate vast amounts of data into abstract concepts and understand data-based reasoning.

- ✔ **New-Media Literacy** ~ ability to critically assess and develop content that uses new media forms and to leverage these media for persuasive communication.

Section 3: Organizational Leadership

✔ **Transdisciplinarity** ~ literacy in and ability to understand concepts across multiple disciplines.

✔ **Design Mindset** ~ ability to represent and develop tasks and work processes for desired outcomes.

✔ **Cognitive Load Management** ~ ability to discriminate and filter information for importance and to understand how to maximize cognitive functioning using a variety of tools and techniques.

✔ **Virtual Collaboration** ~ ability to work productively, drive engagement, and demonstrate presence as a member of a virtual team.

What immediately struck me was the most common element to all ten skills. In some way, they all require an understanding of meaning and context of what is going on around us. In other words, we have to be much more adept at managing knowledge as opposed to merely managing information. Knowledge is information in context so, as the title suggests, our ability to make knowledge-based decisions is crucial to our sustained success as leaders. When we look at new media today, the amount of information we have access to doubles less than every ten minutes. The ability to produce meaningful context (knowledge) from all this information is the difference between progress and failure to meet desired outcomes.

So, how do we develop these ten skills as leaders and as members of the future workforce? In my own experience, these three attitudes are the key to knowledge-based leadership:

✔ **Get comfortable with change faster than traditional business cycles** ~ There are too many changes inside of a twelve-month period for us to wait for the next year to react. If you wait that long, you are already behind!

Section 3: Organizational Leadership

✔ **Be crystal clear on your picture of success** ~ Focusing on a direction helps engage the entire organization in the "What does this mean for us?" discussion. Being a continuous lifelong learner helps in this effort as well!

✔ **Quickly eliminate the noise** ~ If we allow it, information overload clouds our ability to create meaning relevant to our business! The more focus you have, the easier it is to disregard the chaff.

In order to rebalance the gap between too much information and not enough knowledge, leaders must always discern the meaning of what is going on in and around their organization.

So, you have access to all this information. So what?

Lead Well!

Section 3: Organizational Leadership

"Change is inevitable...
growth is optional."

Much has been written about change to the point we can easily and practically understand the impetus of John Maxwell's quote. However, I do not believe enough of those who profess to understand the constant nature of change truly grasp the challenges of growing a business in a constant, fast-paced, changing environment.

So, what does it take to grow in the 21st Century fast-paced global economy? In the March 2014 issue of Inc. Magazine, a Principal Financial Group-sponsored study revealed some simple facts around growing a business.

The first significant finding is, "The only significant predictor of a company's future success is steady growth...Incremental advancement, repeated over time, achieved greater results." The most crucial implication here is that organizational leaders must have a determined and disciplined approach to growing their business.

- ✔ Determined in the form of a plan based on in-depth understanding of who their clients are, what their clients need to succeed, and how the business's products and services meet the client's needs.

- ✔ Disciplined in the form of not being in a way that creates taxing shifts in focus too far from their planned growth path.

The second significant finding is how the identified businesses achieved their steady growth (on average 35% per year for 5 years). The two factors of steady growth are Culture and Employee Engagement. It's been said many times how culture trumps strategy and pretty much anything else it is up against! That is because the culture is the collective beliefs, values, attitudes, behaviors, and norms of the organization. It is easy to see, then, that how people interact and collaborate with each other and with stakeholders is an overall predictor of successful steady growth. So, too, is how well the organization treats its employees by engaging them in the business and compensating them fairly, both monetarily and otherwise. Financial metrics are lagging indicators of success. Only client loyalty, which typically comes on the efforts of fully engaged employees, can be viewed as a leading indicator of success.

Whether you have 2 employees, 200 employees, or 2,000 employees, are for-profit or non-profit, the organization's people are the secret to its success. Ensuring the organization is made up of the right people both in attitude and in skills and knowledge is paramount to steady growth and sustainable success!

How are you leading, and growing, in a determined and disciplined way?

Lead Well!

Section 3: Organizational Leadership

Are you measuring headcount...
or heart-count?

There are times we need remind ourselves as leaders of the importance of engaging followers at a level much deeper than merely following orders. We've all read the ever-growing number of articles and blogs concerning the low levels of employee engagement in the workforce. One reason may well be the simple reference to people as "headcount." What if we stopped measuring headcount and started measuring "heartcount"?

Heartcount, for purposes of this discussion, refers to the level of commitment to the Vision, Mission, and Strategy as active participants in the organizational Culture. Imagine a monthly meeting where leaders report their heartcount or heartcount-as-a-percentage-of-headcount to their management and boards. Think of the discussion that comes out of a leader stating, "We had a 43% heartcount this past quarter" which is akin to saying, "We were 43% committed to the success of the organization this past quarter." As ridiculous as it sounds, that is exactly what the research tells us is happening regardless of how we phrase it!

So how do leaders influence heartcount? While it may seem obvious, the first step is to give the organization something to be committed to. Is the Vision compelling? Is the Mission clear enough to break down the Vision into tangible components? Does the Strategy make sense throughout the organization so that everyone knows how their role influences the overall success? People need something to be committed to in order to be fully engaged!

Set and reinforce expectations. An expectation I reinforced throughout my corporate leadership career was, "I expect 100% out of 100%." In other words, if you see a way to improve the business, you have an obligation to speak up. This philosophy became the catalyst for the culture and promoted commitment to each other throughout the organization.

Section 3: Organizational Leadership

Exercise integrity each day, every day. People can more easily commit to an organization that has true integrity. When leaders commit to their own Beliefs, Attitudes, and Behaviors, the organization will follow suit. Making the right personnel selection decisions (into or out of the organization) that align with the culture and maintaining the integrity of the Vision, Mission, and Strategy is crucial to sustainable heartcount.

Headcount means we have the physical bodies to do the work. Heartcount means we have a commitment to the work leading to sustainable success!

What is your heartcount, and how do you know?

Lead Well!

Section 3: Organizational Leadership

"The culture of any organization is shaped...
by the worst behavior the leader is willing to tolerate."

Why does the situation described in this undated quote by Gruenter and Whitaker occur, and how can leaders avoid this trap? As Peter Drucker says, "Culture eats strategy for breakfast," which means when you get culture right, the rest will, more often than not, fall into place.

Our conversation begins with the definition of culture itself. We define culture as the shared set of beliefs, values, attitudes, behaviors, and norms that guide the behavior of the organization. Every organization, large or small, has a culture that is created in one of three ways:

✔ Leaders hire associates who feel the same way the leader does.

✔ Existing associates are socialized into the leader's way of thinking.

✔ The leader's behaviors act as examples for the organization.

The question is whether the culture exists by design or by circumstance. A culture defined and nurtured by design means the organization's leaders can explicitly define the culture to anyone who asks in very clear and concise terms. They can tell you what their culture is in terms of the specific attitudes and behaviors they expect and routinely hold the organization accountable to. A simple two-question set I use in my coaching practice goes something like:

✔ How do you define your culture? (I am looking for clarity and no hesitation.)

✔ What does that look like? (I am looking for concrete examples of attitude and behavior.)

The ability to answer these two questions in clear and concise terms means the organization's leaders at all levels created a culture that exists by design and with purpose!

Section 3: Organizational Leadership

Of course, the inability to answer these two questions in exact terms, or at all, means the culture exists by circumstance. It exists as a culmination of accepting the worst attitudes and behaviors within the organization. Without definition and accountability, the culture merely becomes the sum of its parts. When the parts are average and mediocre, the culture will reflect that as a whole.

So why do leaders who are quick to say they will not lead average or mediocre businesses do so in spite of themselves? It begins with their inability to define and follow through with specific attitudes and behaviors they expect from themselves and their followers. A leader who says they value their associates and then does nothing about a bully is out of integrity relative to culture. A leader who says they have a culture of collaboration and then accepts results at any cost is out of integrity relative to culture. Being out of integrity means the leader's attitudes, words, and actions are out of sync and violates the very definition of a successful culture.

In Lewis Carroll's *Alice in Wonderland*, the Cheshire Cat says to Alice, "If you do not know where you are going, any road will get you there." If business owners and leaders cannot define their desired culture of success, they end up tolerating average and mediocre associates, suppliers, and even customers who hold them back from achieving their desired results.

How do you define the culture of your business, and what does your culture look like?

Lead Well!

Section 3: Organizational Leadership

When things start going wrong...
do not forget your main goal is to fly the plane.

When I was learning to become a licensed pilot in Alaska as a teenager, part of the process was learning what to do when something goes wrong with the plane. Instead of only talking about what I would do in a given situation, I had to actually demonstrate what to do in any given emergency situation to the flight instructor proving I could do the right thing. That way, when I was faced with the reality of trouble, I knew exactly what to do. Practicing how to recover from stalls (when the plane won't stay in the air) and emergency landings are a normal part of learning to fly. No matter what the challenge, one thing a pilot can never forget while troubleshooting the problem; keep flying the airplane! In the same way, a leader must never forget to keep leading when faced with challenges and issues in the business, even while trying to figure out what to do next.

Based on my experiences with flying, these are three additional lessons I have integrated into my leadership practice over the years:

- ✔ **File a Flight Plan** ~ Before every planned flight, pilots declare a destination and file a flight plan documenting their intended route to reach their destination. This way, someone else knows where the pilot was headed. If something happens, they know where to start looking. Effective business leaders know and understand the value a written and well-communicated plan contributes to the organization's ability to execute. A plane is never exactly on course during the flight, but it is always adjusting to a declared destination. A business is never exactly on plan, yet effective leaders are piloting their teams to achieve desired results!

- ✔ **Use All Your Resources** ~ Pilots have a plethora of resources both internally in the plane and externally on the ground to ensure they have a successful flight. Internally, the instruments let the pilot know how everything is working and if the plane is flying as it should. Externally, the control tower, flight service stations, and other pilots provide additional information in real-time to keep them on course. Effective business leaders also know how to leverage the full capability of their internal resources to provide the information they need to make effective leadership decisions. They also rely on external feedback to ensure they are still on a competitive course in their respective markets and industries!

✓ **Keep Learning** ~ The physics of flying are fundamentally the same. whether you fly a two-seat Cessna or a Boeing 747. All planes fly using the same three axes of yaw, pitch, and roll. Effective pilots always look for ways to improve their flying based on the different conditions they encounter. Learning to fly in Alaska, the weather conditions could change in minutes dramatically altering the flying experience. So, too, effective leaders are constantly developing their leadership skills, knowledge, and attitudes to be adaptable and effective in a myriad of operational situations. Whether you are a small business owner, a non-profit leader, or lead a global corporation, the physics of business are fundamentally the same, yet the context of how these fundamentals are applied changes daily. Effective leaders know how to respond based on their attitude of continuous learning!

Being an effective pilot requires focus, practice, and keeping distractions from getting in the way of your destination. Effective leaders focus on their game plan, never miss an opportunity to practice and refine their leadership craft, and keep distractions from getting in the way of achieving their desired results!

How is your current leadership altitude and course heading?

Lead Well!

Section 3: Organizational Leadership

Change the narrative...
change the culture!

I recently attended a lecture with the above title and was intrigued by the ensuing discussion around how effective communications can literally change the course of an organization based on the narrative used to inspire it. In my mind, effective communication is the number one leadership challenge in business (for-profit and non-profit) today supported by an abundance of real-world examples, surveys, and professional articles. Most surveys I've read on this topic not only identify the issue but also identify leadership's own poor attempts to improve communications within their organizations. It is this challenge to improve what is a well-known issue that highlights this leadership discussion.

Effective communication is defined as the ability of the sender and the receiver to understand the message in the same context. This implies using clarity in the message itself, choosing the most effective and efficient media to transmit the message, and using an effective feedback channel to ensure collective meaning. It all really begins with the clarity of the message itself.

Clarity can be a confusing concept as different people have their own views of how to communicate clearly. An engineer or accountant's view of clarity might involve a heavy dose of facts and figures to clearly identify the core logical message. An artist or designer's view of clarity might involve a heavy dose of flowery and descriptive language to identify the core emotional message. In both cases, the senders are convicted to the clarity of their message. In both cases, some of the receivers have no idea what the core message is!

The solution is the same in both examples. In both scenarios, the messages are full of information without adequate context to understand its meaning. When speakers wrap a narrative around their facts or emotions, they paint a clear picture in the minds of their audience. This is crucial, because, while we hear words, we think in pictures. If a leader wants their narrative to have full effect and meaning, they must tell the story in a way that ensures the picture is the one they intend.

Section 3: Organizational Leadership

How does this, then, impact culture? Culture is the collective beliefs, values, attitudes, behaviors, and norms of the organization. Organizational cultures exist with or without the leader's conscious involvement. The question isn't whether the culture exists, but whether the existing culture is one that will sustainably grow the organization. When a leader determines the culture needs to change to meet evolving business needs (which is always!), they must first look at their own narrative. What are they communicating, both verbally and non-verbally? Are the non-verbal communications aligned and consistent with the verbal communications? What behaviors does the leader expect the team to execute as a result of the their narrative?

The leadership challenge is clear; a constantly changing environment means a constantly evolving narrative in order to achieve sustainable success!

What pictures are your followers envisioning from your leadership narrative?

Lead Well!

Section 3: Organizational Leadership

You don't know SWOT!

Of the many lessons I've learned throughout my career, one that has generated sustainable success is the effective use of the SWOT Analysis. For those readers who are not familiar with the SWOT Analysis, it is a flexible tool that helps the leader identify internal Strengths and Weaknesses as well as external Opportunities and Threats (hence the acronym). It can be used to assess individual circumstances and/or organizational situations with a very straightforward process. The challenges for both frequent SWOT users or those leaders just getting started with the tool is that most fail to realize the full value of the SWOT process. Most only realize half the value by ignoring the most effective part of the tool!

In a traditional SWOT Analysis, the leader creates four lists containing the collective insights on the internal Strengths (list #1) and Weaknesses (list #2) along with the external Opportunities (list #3) and Threats (list #4). More often than not, these lists contain anywhere from a half-dozen entries to well over twenty entries, depending on the circumstances. A more experienced SWOT user will realize each list should be no more than five entries due to the need to truly focus on the most important elements in each list. Even this is not enough as these lists now sit embedded in a strategic planning document or a project plan without providing any context to the leader.

The secret to deriving full value from the SWOT Analysis is to synthesize the four lists into a strategic matrix that reflects the contextual relationship between the Strengths, Weaknesses, Opportunities, and Threats into a single view. The leader forms the matrix by listing the top five Strengths and Weaknesses across the top of the matrix and the top five Opportunities and Threats down the left side of the matrix. This creates an opportunity to complete a two-by-two matrix where the four lists intersect. The leader completes each of the intersecting sections in a way that identifies actions that will:

Section 3: Organizational Leadership

- ✓ …leverage their internal competitive Strengths in order to capitalize on key external Opportunities (Strengths/Opportunities)

- ✓ …use their internal competitive Strengths to minimize external competitive Threats (Strengths/Threats)

- ✓ …minimize or eliminate perceived internal Weaknesses while making the most of any new external Opportunities (Weaknesses/Opportunities)

- ✓ …minimize an organization's internal Weaknesses while at the same time minimize external Threats (Weaknesses/Threats)

After completing each of these four new sections of the matrix, the leader can now review the full SWOT Synthesis to determine the most appropriate strategic objectives for them personally or the organization they lead. The SWOT Synthesis becomes the supporting narrative for why certain strategies become the focus based on the analysis/synthesis process. With effective use of the SWOT Analysis and Synthesis combination, the Strategic priorities practically write themselves!

How well do you know SWOT and what does it say about your organization's priorities?

Lead Well!

Section 3: Organizational Leadership

A business does well...
what its leaders measure.

One of the challenges in today's business environment is the ability to show measurable progress in every one of the business's endeavors. Entrepreneurs wear so many hats they struggle with where to focus their metrics. Non-profit leaders get caught up in activities without understanding their measurable impact. Corporate leaders create a false sense of security because they only see the business through report-driven metrics. I mention all of this to get to a simple question, "How do you know your business is achieving desired results?"

For me, the best answer has always included using the Balanced Scorecard approach introduced by Robert Kaplan and David Norton in their 1996 book *The Balanced Scorecard: Translating Strategy into Action*. Regardless of the measurement tool and/or philosophy you use, there are two tenets I use when helping clients identify areas of process improvement and quality that belong in any discussion of measuring success:

✔ **Measure to Capture the Whole Story ~** When leaders look for validation of progress and/or success, their most convenient option is the pile of reports or data housed in the many systems at their disposal. Technology provides a world where they have seemingly unlimited access to data and information. However, it is the conclusions leaders draw from that information that matters most in understanding their proximity to success. A heavy reliance on objective information limits their effectiveness as business

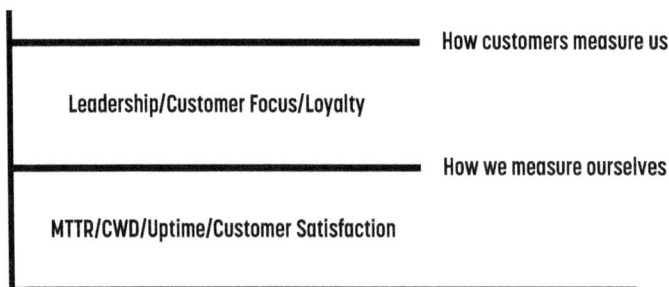

How customers measure us

Leadership/Customer Focus/Loyalty

How we measure ourselves

MTTR/CWD/Uptime/Customer Satisfaction

Section 3: Organizational Leadership

We had a plethora of objective measures resulting in multiple pages of information on how we were performing against our own metrics. However, we only had an inkling of what that meant to our clients! Until we added the focus on balancing our metrics with feedback from the clients themselves, the decisions we made had limited value. Combining the voice of the customer with internally focused metrics, leaders have a more complete understanding of performance which means that the decisions they make are more impactful to sustainable success!

✓ **Measure Quality in the Correct Sequence** ~ How many times do leaders hear and accept the following as they dissect a process issue? "I turned in the contract on time…" "I submitted the order just like the process says…" "I wrote it down just as the client said…" By taking these statements, and others like them, at face value, the leader often misidentifies the issue at hand. The question is not whether the information was provided but whether it was provided correctly and completely so the next step in the process was set up for success. Using an example from my own experience, account executives (sales reps) submit contracts for new deals sold following a process to ensure the contract gets processed accurately so the client is billed correctly. However, when the billing is wrong, the tendency is to look at the billing department when the process started at the account executive. Allowing sales to submit incomplete or incorrect information means the process is dead on arrival. The diagram below is of a simple process (Supplier, Input, Process Tasks, Output, and Consumer).

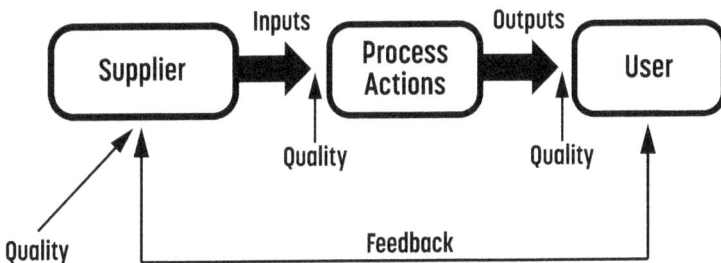

Section 3: Organizational Leadership

Notice the quality measurement points are where the inputs and outputs meet the next step in the process. In the previous example with sales contracts, the only valid place to determine if quality metrics were met would be with the contract administration team who received the sales contracts from the sales team. We switched our thinking and provided a quality report to the Vice President of Sales, so the quality and the quantity of sales orders were measured and reviewed. When the quality of orders goes up, the billing issues decrease and profits increase. When leaders measure quality in the correct sequence, true quality becomes integral to sustained success!

Regardless of industry, type, or size of business, measuring progress is a key leadership role and imperative to sustainable success. No matter how much data technology provides a leader, the Voice of the Customer must always factor into the leader's business decisions. Inherent in those decisions is the Quality of inputs and outputs, both internal and external, to the business. Keeping these two key tenets in mind will help leaders at all levels make better business decisions!

How well is your business progressing, and how do you know?

Lead Well!

Section 3: Organizational Leadership

The invention of the ship...
was also the invention of the shipwreck!

Effective leadership involves, among other things, a sound decision-making process. This process involves looking at not only a decision's immediate impact but the longer-term effects as well. As this quote from French philosopher, urbanist, and cultural theorist Paul Virilio suggests, there is casualty in every leadership decision. For context, the decisions discussed here are primarily focused on ones with the broadest impact to the organization and the strategy. Understanding the impact decisions have in a broader sense is a challenge every leader faces multiple times a day!

- ✔ **There are always Pros and Cons ~** The first thing to understand is that every decision has pros and cons. It seems obvious, yet I routinely see leaders making decisions only based on the upside of their decision, falling victim to their own confirmation biases. I see this regularly as part of a case study assignment I give to MBA students. Part of the assignment involves identifying the pros and cons of decisions within the case study. The number one reason these future leaders lose points is only listing the pros of the decision when it clearly states to list both the pros and cons in the syllabus. Time and again, what they perceive to be the right approach falls short by not considering the negative as well as the positive consequences of key leadership decisions!

- ✔ **Managing Risk ~** Suffice it to say, most decisions at this level have a degree of risk based on the pros and cons. The leader's attitude toward risk will influence how the final decision is made. I suspect that if those who did invent the ship had known about shipwrecks, they still would not have changed their decision. 21st Century leaders are challenged with having to make decisions based on the pros while knowing the cons, which should have minimal impact relative to the advantages (pros) of the decisions.

Section 3: Organizational Leadership

- ✔ **Impact of Pace** ~ Once leaders have identified the pros and cons and have come to terms with their risk tolerance, they factor the impact of pace. Simply stated, the speed of business does not allow unbounded time to confer, deliberate, and reflect on key decisions. As leaders will never have enough time to do all they want to do (hence the need for priorities), they will rarely have enough time to make the perfect decision. When leaders complain to me about not having enough time (which is very common), my response to them is to know their business well enough to be able to quickly put key decisions into context. Routinely receiving feedback from their team is crucial to a continuous business knowledge process such that only a small amount of additional information is needed at decision-making time to make the best decision for the organization!

Effective leadership decision-making is both an art and a science. It involves looking at both short-term and long-term impacts on the organization and making tough decisions even with an occasional shipwreck as part of the impact!

Is your next decision a ship, a shipwreck, or a little bit of both, and how do you know?

Lead Well!

Section 3: Organizational Leadership

You never truly believe in something...
until you have to believe in something.

In this day and age of information overload and social media sharing hundreds of opinions a second, it is becoming increasingly difficult to truly know what an organization believes in. We often know what the business leaders say they believe, just like we hear religious leaders, politicians, and name-your-influencers state their beliefs. But how do we really know what is talk and what is ground truth? How should followers know what the organization's leaders believe, and what impact does it have on leadership?

We work and live in an environment where causes have a much greater impact on the way business is conducted than in the previous century. B Corporations, the Triple Bottom Line, Cause Marketing, and Social Enterprise are terms that, while not new in their creation, are relatively new to the mainstream business lexicon. In the last several years, we've seen cases that we characterize into two main categories; those organizations where the belief system is reinforced from the top down and those organizations where the belief system is reinforced from the bottom up.

- ✓ **Top-down beliefs ~** It is no secret that Patagonia, the outerwear company that started by making equipment for climbers, is now fully vested in their business model around being eco-friendly. Their mission statement is clear, "We're in business to save our home planet." While many companies say they are eco-friendly, Patagonia puts their money where their mouth is, as evidenced most recently by donating their entire $10M 2018 tax benefit to organizations that work to save the planet!

- ✓ **Bottom-up beliefs ~** Any company that does business with the federal government is certainly open to opinion and critique due to the open nature of government contracts. So, it is no surprise that Microsoft employees had access to the purpose of some of the augmented reality software they normally would use for gaming being developed for the government. There was a groundswell of resistance to supporting the $480M contract as employees felt the software could also be used to "help kill people" leading to a petition to the CEO of Microsoft asking him back out of the contract!

Regardless of personal opinions on these two examples, they demonstrate the risk and reward of having strong beliefs backed by words and even more powerful the beliefs backed by actions, whether they come from the top or the bottom.

When working with clients on values, we ask them to consider a situation where they need to publicly support their point of view. For example, if a person is opposed to gay marriage due to religious reasons (a topic that is discussed in the workplace), we might ask, "What would you tell someone if the gay person was your own son or daughter?" By making the beliefs personal, it helps that leader not only address their beliefs from a distance but also from an up close and empathetic point of view. This process may or may not change their personal point of view, but, at a minimum, it provides a depth of understanding of their own point of view and conviction of belief as a leader.

What do you believe in, and how do you know?

Lead Well!

Section 3: Organizational Leadership

"There is nothing so useless...
as doing efficiently what should not be done at all."

I spend a good bit of time in my practice working with businesses on their business planning and people development initiatives. A few of these clients have also invested their time in what is likely the least appreciated part of achieving sustainable success in business ~ process improvement! Peter Drucker's quote above is a reminder to all business leaders, regardless of business size, industry, or profit status, that everything we do is a process, and we should well be aware of whether we are doing the *right things* well versus just doing *anything* well.

All successful organizations use the same basic processes regardless of whether they sell services, products, or both. Core processes are ones that directly influence revenue acquisition. Supporting processes are those that have an indirect influence on revenue acquisition. These supporting processes include functions such as Human Resources, Information Technology, Research & Development, and General Administration, to name a few. Let's focus on the five Core Processes that all businesses use and see how they impact your business:

- ✔ **Supply Chain Management** ~ all processes associated with the inbound logistics of the business such as materials, inventory, and consumables associated with the input to your business operations. How are you measuring the quality of what comes into your business?

- ✔ **Operations** ~ all processes associated with converting the inputs from the supply chain processes into creating the products and services the business provides. How do you know you are producing the quality expected by your customers?

- ✔ **Distribution** ~ all processes associated with the distribution of your products and/or services to the buyers. If the buyer is not the end user, how well is your product or service being received by the end user?

- ✓ **Sales and Marketing** ~ all processes associated with the advertising, promotion, and sale of your products and/or services. How well is your brand known in the market, and how profitable is your sales process?

- ✓ **Customer Service** ~ all processes associated with providing service and ongoing assistance and support of your products and/or services to buyers. What is the overall experience of your buyers, and how do you know?

Whenever we work with a growing business, we look specifically at these five core processes in the context of the client's business model and growth plan. This is especially true with small businesses or non-profits who may not yet have these processes in place. In all cases, when we addressed these five core processes by creating and documenting how they should work, the growth of the business was much easier to manage and scale.

Process improvement is not just for bigger businesses with lots of resources to manage how they run their business. Poor processes can derail even the best business plan and ruin even the best people if not given the structure to succeed!

What is your business doing well that it shouldn't be doing at all, and how do you know?

Lead Well!

Section 3: Organizational Leadership

"Strap yourselves in…
we're going to jump to light speed!"

I still remember the audience's reaction to this scene in the *Star Wars: A New Hope* in 1977. We had never seen anything like it on the big screen until then and, of course, now it seems almost archaic! Today's 21st Century business environment can feel very much like everything is moving at perpetual light speed. Simply stated, it is not the ability to adapt that matters as much as the speed at which the leader is able to adapt in order to stay relevant. Here are three things a 21st Century leader can do to stay relevant:

- ✔ **How well do you know your industry?** ~ While I was once asked if I had a crystal ball to see the future, no one has that ability. However, we do have the ability to understand our industry well enough to understand key trends and how those trends impact the leader's current and future business. In the May-June 2018 issue of *Harvard Business Review*, Jason Trujillo, IBM's Director of Leadership Development, sums up this dynamic with one sentence. He states, "IBM's cultural transformation is aligned with the reinvention of our business, with almost half our revenue coming from businesses we weren't in six years ago." Six years to a company as large as IBM is virtually light speed!

- ✔ **Excellence is not the same as perfect!** ~ Contrary to what many believe based on their actions, a leader can lead with excellence without being perfect. Actually, the desire to be perfect or make perfect decisions will slow the process down, not speed it up. Making decisions with 85% of the necessary information puts the team well ahead of those leaders waiting to be perfect with 100% of the information. The truth is, by the time 100% of the information is collected for the decision, the original context has likely changed.

Section 3: Organizational Leadership

- ✓ **What are you willing to proactively change, and how frequent are you willing to change?** ~ Knowing it's important to adapt is one thing, choosing to take action is another thing altogether. Leaders who adapt well know what needs to change and are not afraid to act on those needs with purpose. When I first announced to my teams we would change something every six months, the resistance was palpable. After several cycles of six-month changes, the teams realized the value of the new pace, and those that stayed willingly embraced it as the "new normal"!

It is not just the ability to adapt, it is the ability to adapt quickly and, preferably, ahead of industry trends that leads to success. Waiting for the market to dictate how you run your business means your business will hover on average, missing the opportunity to be excellent!

What are you going to change next as a leader?

Lead Well!

Section 3: Organizational Leadership

"If you want to understand how a lion hunts...
don't go to the zoo. Go to the jungle."

This quote by Jim Stengel, former Chief Marketing Officer at Proctor & Gamble, sets up this discussion as we explore the importance of effectively communicating diverse thinking to adapt and stay relevant.

It is my contention that effective communication is the biggest challenge 21st Century leaders face today! When we think consider the ramifications of poor leadership communications, we can clearly see why this is such a big issue. What can leaders do to effectively communicate at the speed of business?

- ✓ **Knowledge Rules** ~ Technology gives us easy, unfettered access to vast amounts of data and information. That said, leaders who rely too heavily on information for their business decisions are missing a crucial element of success ~ Knowledge! Knowledge is information in context. In other words, it applies meaning to information which makes what the information we have more useful and effective. Where content is 'how and what,' knowledge is 'where when' that information has relevance to the discussion at hand.

- ✓ **Communicate Meaning** ~ Effective communications, by definition, occurs when the sender and the receiver understand the message in the same context. Essentially, it is sharing meaning, not just words or images, to convey an idea or expectation. Far too many leaders are communicating content that is open to multiple interpretations by their followers. Multiple interpretations lead to confusion and, ultimately, failure in achieving the message's desired results. Effective leaders communicate content and context to eliminate these multiple interpretations and ensure mutual understanding of the actions necessary for execution. To do this effectively, leaders know it takes time as well as a deeper understanding of the business, industry, and markets. Leaders must adapt their communication style to ensure knowledge-based mutual understanding!

- ✓ **Real-Time Context Matters ~** Much has been written about the millions of dollars wasted in ineffective leadership development programs. One of the primary reasons is that, for the most part, they are not development programs at all, rather, they are training programs disguised as development. To truly be an effective leadership development program, the skills (content) have to be applied in the context of the leader's role. This gives meaning (context) to the content so that new leadership habits and attitudes can develop when applied effectively over time. It takes time as well as a conscious focus to achieve results, but the payoff is being able to effectively lead at the speed of business!

Thanks to technology, the amount of information we have access to increases at an exponential rate. In many cases, leaders are literally looking for the knowledge needle in the information haystack! However, what leaders do with the information available to them is far more important that the information they've accumulated over time. Anyone can search for information on the internet. It is knowing what to do with the information, or whether it is, in fact, the right information, that allows effective leaders to make the right knowledge-based decisions at the speed of business!

How are you learning how the lion hunts?

Lead Well!

Section 3: Organizational Leadership

What we see...
depends mainly on what we look for.

It seems that articles and blog posts on the importance of culture to business success can be found just about everywhere you look in business industry publications. With all the expertise being distributed, you have to wonder why we haven't figured it out by now! The key lies in how we define culture combined with the accelerated speed of change we now face as 21st Century leaders.

I define culture as the shared beliefs, values, attitudes, behaviors, and norms that guide members of the organization. Based on this definition, we can conclude that culture exists in every organization, large or small. While every organization has culture embedded in its DNA, the real question is whether the culture can support sustainable success through the vision and strategy of the business. How does a leader know if the culture is what they want it to be?

✔ **Define the Culture** ~ Too many leaders talk the talk of culture yet struggle to define their own business cultures. If we go back to the definition, a culture is defined by a set of attitudes and behaviors any outsider could see and describe. This is not as easy as it sounds, especially when describing the attitudes desired in the culture. If a leader tells me their culture is one of "can-do," then what does that look like?

✔ **Audit the Culture** ~ Once defined, leaders periodically plug into the culture and see if it is what they believe it to be. The title quote of this article by John Lubbock speaks to leaders who can offer a litany of things done to create the desired culture without spending the requisite time validating their efforts. Culture is defined by what the organization's members do, not by what the leader wants them to do!

Section 3: Organizational Leadership

- ✔ **Live the Culture ~** The leader's most important task is setting an example of the culture they have defined by demonstrating it in action. Living the culture with integrity means the leaders themselves are living examples to the organization of the desired attitudes and behaviors expected by everyone in the business. It does little good to espouse the virtues of a family-oriented culture if leaders treat associates as expendable laborers whose only value is in the transactions they conduct. Their behavior will dictate the culture.

- ✔ **Hire for Cultural Fit ~** The last piece of this discussion is hiring people who are a cultural fit to the organization. Once again, the definition of culture comes into play when new associates are predominantly hired for their attitudes and values. While skills and knowledge are important, they only represent a quarter of the success of the new hire. Attitude represents the majority of the cultural fit and is what the leader must be looking for in the hiring process. Having used this successfully in my own career, I continue to see examples of success when attitude is the differentiator over skills and knowledge, even when the skills are less than what is initially desired.

I often use a graphic of an iceberg to depict culture. The behaviors are the tip that we see above the water. The remaining elements of the culture (values, attitudes, beliefs, etc.) lie with the rest (over 90%) of the iceberg, below the waterline where it cannot be seen. To accurately define the culture, leaders must look deeper to get a full picture.

What do others see in your culture?

Lead Well!

Appendix A

Results!

The Business Alignment Maturity Model ©

The Business Alignment Maturity Model ©
[BAMM] provides a successful framework for achieving the improved results all effective leaders strive for.

Operating without it is like trying to complete a thousand piece puzzle without the picture on the box. It might get done but it will take far longer to finish.

Each layer must align to the layer below it prior to moving to the next layer.

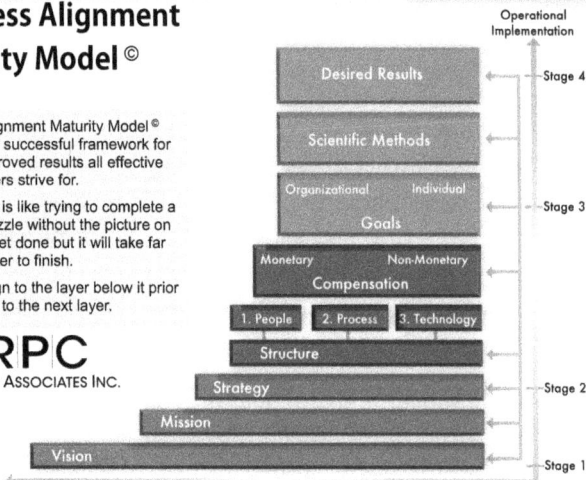

RPC
LEADERSHIP ASSOCIATES INC.

Operational Implementation

Desired Results — Stage 4

Scientific Methods

Organizational   Individual
Goals — Stage 3

Monetary   Non-Monetary
Compensation

1. People   2. Process   3. Technology

Structure

Strategy — Stage 2

Mission

Vision — Stage 1

Results!

The Business Alignment Maturity Model ©

Vision – Your Vision outlines the organizational or personal direction for the future. Think of it as your "North Star" for the next 5 years.

Mission – Your Mission Statement adds more specificity to how you will accomplish your Vision over the next 2 to 3 years.

Strategy – Your Strategy speaks to how you will execute against your competition or your personal barriers during this business cycle (typically this current year).

Structure – Most organizations are organized vertically around processes that work horizontally. Structural alignment occurs when People, Processes and Technology work with the Strategy, not at cross-purposes with it.

1. People: Organizations must continuously assess whether their people are capable and compatible with the Strategy, especially as it evolves.

2. Process: It is said that bad processes can ruin good people. Organizations must align their processes with the right people not the other way around.

3. Technology: Technology supports people and process. Organizations must ensure their technology is supporting, not inhibiting the Strategy.

Compensation – Since Success comes from a positive change in Behaviors and Habits, how will you incent the right behaviors for your organization and/or yourself?

Goals – These are specific and detailed objectives required to successfully execute the Strategy. They are accompanied by Action Steps to outline in detail Who does What by When.

Scientific Methods – Along with Who, What and When you also need to determine How you will measure your progress toward your Strategy.

Results – The culmination of your planning and execution! The Business Alignment Model helps you articulate the Results in the context of your Strategy and ultimately your overall Vision.

About the Author

Rick Lochner is the President and CEO of RPC Leadership Associates, Inc. He is an accomplished Coach, Facilitator, College Professor, Keynote and Workshop Speaker, Author, and, foremost, a Leader.

The Vision of RPC Leadership Associates, Inc. is to help Business Owners, Corporate and Non-Profit Leadership Teams, and Individual Professionals Make Leadership a Way of Life. He and his associates coach organizational leaders to leverage effective goal-setting, organizational planning, people development, and process improvement to ensure their business strategies achieve their desired results.

Rick is a graduate of the United States Military Academy at West Point and spent his 11-year military career leading soldiers in challenging environments around the globe. After leaving the Army, he spent the next 18 years in corporate leadership positions ranging from front-line management to senior executive management. He successfully led organizations in Fortune 100 corporations and privately held entrepreneurizal ventures across multiple industries.

In addition to his undergraduate studies, Rick holds both an MS and MBA. He is an Adjunct Professor at Aurora University where he teaches a variety of leadership-related topics including 21st Century Leadership, Managing Organizational Change, and Strategic Management.

In addition to publishing *I'm Just Sayin'… Revelations for Making Leadership a Way of Life* in 2014, he is also the author of *The Missing Piece* series of books for Entrepreneurs, Non-Profit Leaders, and Corporate Leaders applying the Business Alignment Maturity Model to achieve sustainable organizational success.

Rick gives back to the local community as a mentor and coach for the local school district INCubator program as well as facilitating the nationally recognized Rising Stars Leadership Development Program for local high school Sophomores and Juniors. He and his wife, Colleen, reside in Naperville, IL.

Thank You!